A Red Sea
RISING
The Flood of the Century

Winnipeg Free Press

Winnipeg, Manitoba
1997

A RED SEA
RISING
The Flood of the Century

© Copyright 1997 Winnipeg Free Press
All rights reserved
ISBN 0-9682575-0-X
Printed in Canada

CANADIAN CATALOGUING IN PUBLICATION DATA

Main entry under title:

A red sea rising: the flood of the century

       Includes index.
       ISBN 0-9682575-0-X
       1. Floods – Red River Valley (Minn. and N.D.-Man.)
       2. Manitoba – History

GB1399.5.C3R43 1997   971.27'403   C97-900965-0

First printing September, 1997
Second printing October, 1997
Third printing November, 1977

Front cover photo by Ken Gigliotti: Randy Garriock helps Dale Dabrowski, closest to boat, clear out Dabrowski's home near St. Adolphe on April 25.
Back cover photo by Marc Gallant: Glenlawn Collegiate student Kris Pikl sandbags on Christie Road on April 21.

Dedication

This book is dedicated
to the people of Manitoba
who faced the challenge
of the Red River
in the spring of 1997.

Table of Contents

Preface

We were reminded again this year of two immutable truths: the awesome power of Mother Nature and the indomitable spirit of the human family. Manitobans and their friends responded with impressive determination as the overflowing Red River tested our resolve and capacity to withstand its onslaught.

Watching Manitobans of all ages and from every walk of life band together in common cause was reminiscent of another spring in the Red River Valley 47 years ago, at a time when our defences were not so strong. It was during the devastating flood of 1950, when I was throwing sandbags and organizing other volunteers to combat the surging waters of the Red, that it became clear that we needed more than earthen dikes to protect our community. Along with other Manitobans, I breathed a great sigh of relief when the floodway did its job and protected the vast majority of Winnipeg's citizens and their homes. The performance of that structure of steel and concrete was matched by the truly inspirational role played by the men, women and children who dropped everything to beat back the threat of the rising river. It is at moments such as these when the very best of a community's character comes to the fore.

Private citizens did their job and so did governments at all levels. The steady flow of information from civic and provincial officials kept a nervous population calm and well informed. The comforting presence of the Canadian armed forces reminded us that we are not alone, that we arc part of a larger community that responds with speed and efficiency when one of its own is in distress. Just as the flood of '97 brought out the best in Manitobans, so did it release an outpouring of support, moral and material, from our fellow citizens in every region of Canada.

While our defences are strong and our determination solid, there is still work to be done. Let the lessons of 1997 lead to a better way, just as the costly legacy of 1950 propelled us into action a decade later.

I also want to compliment and thank the *Winnipeg Free Press* for its excellent coverage of the flood story. The newspaper that is so much a part of our province's past, continues to serve the community today.

This fine book will offer a permanent reminder that when nature challenges us, Manitobans, with a little help from their friends, will summon the will to meet it.

Duff Roblin

Foreword

T he great flood of 1997 was the biggest story that many of us at the *Winnipeg Free Press* had ever covered. From the moment that the centre of Grand Forks, North Dakota, was destroyed, the newsroom at the *Free Press* switched into a gear that it has probably not been in outside of wartime. For us, there was very little else that mattered. From the outset, we determined to tell Manitobans as much as we possibly could about the threat that faced them in a manner that was calm, collected and as useful as it could possibly be. There was no need to exaggerate a danger that everyone on the paper faced equally with the readers we serve. For more than two weeks, there was very little in the main news section of the *Free Press* other than coverage of the flood.

As the waters subsided, it became clear that the flood had been more than just a big story. It had been a moment in Manitoba history that generations would wish to understand. In the rush of our coverage, we had been unable to explain the detail of the planning, the fear of failure or the magnitude of some of the decisions that were being made day by day.

There was, we knew, a behind-the-scenes drama with its own heroes, arguments, tensions, failures and successes.

No organization was in a better position than the *Free Press* to put that whole story together. Our reporters received enormous co-operation from the key players in explaining what happened and the decisions they made. What follows is the story of how Winnipeg and Manitoba fought a great natural disaster.

NICHOLAS HIRST
Editor
Winnipeg Free Press

Acknowledgment

The people who staff the *Free Press* newsroom must be first in line to be thanked for making this book possible. Almost every staffer had a hand in covering the flood of 1997; those who did not work directly on the flood story made it possible for those who did.

For some of our reporters, editors and photographers, the flood was an all-consuming event for more than a month and one that they will remember as the greatest story of their careers. The stories, photographs and charts they produced on the spot are the major sources for this book. In addition, Kim Guttormson, Bruce Owen, Bill Redekop and Gordon Sinclair Jr. did major research in the aftermath of the flood.

Thanks are also due to the people they interviewed after the crisis had passed. From the provincial government, we particularly appreciate the co-operation of Gary Filmon, Harold Clayton, Ron Richardson, Don Kuryk, Larry Whitney and Alf Warkentin. At city hall, Mayor Susan Thompson and Loren Reynolds were helpful. From the armed forces, Generals Bob Meating and Bruce Jeffries both spoke candidly and at length about their work in Manitoba.

Our proprietor, Thomson Newspapers, supplemented our news budget and encouraged us to spend whatever was necessary to produce the best flood coverage we could manage. We increased the "news hole," the daily allotment of paper for news coverage, and we had a free hand to buy cell phones and portable computers, rent trucks and boats and charter airplanes and helicopters.

BUZZ CURRIE
Features Editor
Winnipeg Free Press

Contributors

The Staff of the Winnipeg Free Press who produced A Red Sea Rising.

BUZZ CURRIE – Features Editor

Currie is the author of A Red Sea Rising. His text brings together information gathered before, during and after the flood of 1997 by the reporting staff of the Winnipeg Free Press.

PAUL PIHICHYN – Assistant Editor,
New Business Development

Pihichyn served as editor of the book and project co-ordinator.

GORDON PREECE – Art Director

Preece was responsible for the design and layout of A Red Sea Rising.

JON THORDARSON – Photo and Graphics Editor

Thordarson selected the photographs used in A Red Sea Rising and served as photo editor. Thordarson was assisted by artist Kittie Wong. Thordarson was responsible for directing the Winnipeg Free Press photo coverage of the 1997 flood.

RON CAMPBELL – Copy Editor

Campbell was the principal copy editor of A Red Sea Rising. He was assisted by other members of the Free Press copy editing staff.

LINDA QUATTRIN – Assistant City Editor

Quattrin wrote the captions for the photographs in A Red Sea Rising.

THE REPORTERS

Gordon Sinclair Jr., Kim Guttormson, Bill Redekop, Bruce Owen, Manfred Jager, with assistance from the reporting staff of the Winnipeg Free Press.

THE PHOTOGRAPHERS

Jon Thordarson, Wayne Glowacki, Phil Hossack, Ken Gigliotti, Jeff DeBooy, Joe Bryksa, Marc Gallant, Boris Minkevich, Randy Turner. Additional photography from The Canadian Press, The Associated Press, Ian McCausland, David Stock.

THE ARTISTS

Gordon Preece and Linda Stilkowski.

A Red Sea Rising: The Flood of the Century is published by the Winnipeg Free Press.
Rudy Redekop – Publisher
Nicholas Hirst – Editor

Printed by Friesen Printers, Altona, Manitoba.

A Red Sea
RISING
The Flood of the Century

Chapter One
THE BLIZZARD

SUNDAY, APRIL 6, 1997 was a day off for most people in the Red River Valley, but it wasn't a standard day of rest. All along the 555 miles of twisting river, from its source in North Dakota to its delta at Lake Winnipeg, there were people who wanted to be at work but were idled by the wind, snow and chill of a prairie blizzard.

Even the most casual of snowbound observers knew the blizzard spelled trouble. Already, there was more snow on the ground than most people could remember seeing – more than 100 inches along the upper reaches of the river and more than 60 inches around Winnipeg. That's about twice the normal thickness of the winter blanket. In the flat-as-a-table Red River Valley, that much snow on the ground at spring thaw could only mean flooding. And now, just as the valley's temperatures began to peek over the freezing level, a massive "Colorado clipper" snowstorm was piling up drifts on top of the drifts.

One of the forcibly idled people was Harold Clayton, stranded in his home in Linden Woods in southwest Winnipeg. Clayton is executive co-ordinator of Manitoba's Emergency Management Organization. Had he been able to get out of his driveway, he'd have gone to his office in the Woodsworth Building, across Broadway from the Manitoba Legislative Building. There was much to do; flooding was already an accepted certainty in the valley. Clayton's office was responsible for co-ordinating the response to that flooding – maintaining the dikes that protected the towns along the river and being ready to move people out of the flood path if evacuation became necessary.

Already, Clayton had been told there was a 10 per cent chance the flood would be as bad as that of 1979. That flood had turned southern Manitoba into a lake 56 miles long from north to south and 12.5 miles across at its widest point. The destruction had been terrible.

Clayton was relatively new in the position; his first day on the job had been August 12, 1996. A 45-year-old former volunteer paramedic with the ambulance department in Portage la Prairie, he had also been

an alderman in that city until the EMO job moved him to Winnipeg. Of medium height, Clayton speaks in a deep, slow voice and frequently pauses to choose his words. The impression is of a man who will not crack easily under pressure.

The swirling snow outside his window told Clayton his problems had multiplied, but not by how much. To find that out, he would need hours at his desk. He would not get to put in any of those hours on this Sunday; the city was virtually shut down. Car travel was impossible, transit buses couldn't move; ambulances got about only with a front-end loader for an escort. Like it or not, Clayton was going to have a day off.

It would be 49 days – not until Sunday, May 25 – before he had another one. In the seven intervening weeks, he would sleep little and he would fight the flood of the century.

Similarly snowbound was one of Clayton's chief sources of information, hydrometeorologist Alf Warkentin. It's Warkentin's job to predict river levels all over Manitoba. He's virtually a one-man operation, practising his arcane craft in a warren of rooms in the Water Resources Branch offices on Dublin Avenue in northwest Winnipeg.

The April 5-6 snowfall (opposite page) was not merely deep – it was lead-heavy. It would melt into millions of cubic feet of water. Plaridel Orcullo digs out on Mountain Avenue after the storm.

Even Portage Avenue was impassable on Sunday afternoon, April 6.

1

"I've had water
in my veins,
so to speak,
since I was
a little boy"
ALF WARKENTIN

Joe Bryksa

Born 55 years ago and raised on a dairy farm near Grunthal, Alfred Warkentin has had a fascination with water for as long as he can remember.

"I've had water in my veins, so to speak, since I was a little boy," he told *Free Press* reporter Bill Redekop in the aftermath of the flood. "I used to go out walking in the fields in my rubber boots and I would watch the overland flooding, watching the directions it would flow."

He attended the University of Manitoba, obtaining a science degree with majors in physics and mathematics. He followed that with a year-long course in meteorology offered by Environment Canada, and went to work weather forecasting with the department the next year.

In a decision the province would never regret, Warkentin was hired. Coincidentally, Warkentin, emergency flood spokesman Larry Whitney, and Rick Bowering, head of Water Resources – three leaders in the battle against the flood of the century – were all hired within a few months of each other in 1970.

Warkentin was 28 when he approached the province about making him its river forecaster. He urged them to adopt the more scientific approach he could give them. At the time, the province's river forecasting was quasi-scientific at best. There was no single person in charge and the procedures in use had been out of date for years.

With no flood forecasting courses in the country, Warkentin began attending seminars and taking courses in hydrology and statistics. In the 27 years since his first day on the job, he has evolved a system, fully understood only by himself, that predicts river levels with uncanny accuracy.

There are 14 tributaries flowing into the Red River in southern Manitoba, including the Assiniboine River, and about 25 in North Dakota and Minnesota. One of Warkentin's biggest tasks is to estimate the daily discharges from those tributaries into the Red River.

Warkentin uses river gauges, precipitation gauges, soil moisture maps, topographical maps, coefficient formulas and historic records to predict watershed runoff volumes and create daily flow charts for tributary discharges into the Red. From the daily discharges he projects river levels and crests up and down the river. He must also factor in overland flooding and future snowfall, melt rates and rain.

He then multiplies his figures against a multiple regression coefficient – a formula for determining how much weight to give each factor. He keeps such analyses for every year dating back to the early 1900s.

Warkentin is fascinated by water in all its manifestations. He includes a lot of water in his diet. He brings distilled water to work in plastic soda pop bottles that end up strewn about his office by the end of the day.

He was there on Saturday, April 5, as the first flakes of the blizzard drifted down about 4 p.m. Warkentin already had more than an inkling that the mounting snowfall would mean a flood unlike any witnessed this century. He made calls to meteorologists in the United States to get rough calculations of the snow's water content. On the way home that night, he got stuck in the parking lot. Already, the wind had hammered the snow and ice pellets into hard-as-iron drifts. The next morning, he called emergency services for a ride to the office, but emergency's manpower was already overtaxed. So Warkentin started making phone calls from home to colleagues in Minnesota and North Dakota. "I realized then we were in real trouble," he said later. "I knew it was going to be a long spring."

Two hundred and fifty miles south, the snow was welcome. Pam Dohman thought it would be a blessed relief from the rain that had been pounding down on her home town of Breckenridge, Minn. The Minnesotans reasoned that snow would pile up and, with luck, melt slowly into the river system.

The Red River forms just across the state line from Breckenridge, in Wahpeton, N.D. There, the Bois de Sioux River coming down from the south is joined by the Ottertail River coming west through

Tammy Lajeunesse (left) notes that Elite Communications on St. James Street is open Monday morning. Slogging down Pembina Highway (far left) on Sunday.

Ken Gigliotti

Ken Gigliotti

Boyd Avenue residents clear their street.

Jeff DeBooy

Sidewalks (far left) are plugged, so Richard Temple hikes down freshly-plowed Portage Avenue. Digging out (left) the day after in Garden Grove.

Joe Bryksa

An intrepid shopper (above) heads for Eaton's warehouse.

TransCanada Highway travellers (right) had their work cut out for them.

Minnesota. The result is what Americans call the Red River of the North, to distinguish it from the Red River in north Texas. Canadians simply call it the Red River.

Dohman was helping co-ordinate volunteer floodfighting as the Red and its tributary streams simultaneously thawed and climbed out of their banks. "We were so prepared," she told *Free Press* reporter Kim Guttormson as the storm gathered on Saturday. "The last 24 hours have been hell."

It got worse. One-and-a-half inches of rain, driven by wind that gusted up to 50 miles an hour, broke through the dikes – levees, Americans call them – late Saturday and the 3,700 people in Breckenridge were moved to Wahpeton. They weren't the first evacuees of the flood of the century, though. That distinction went to the animals in the Wahpeton zoo, moved to higher and dryer ground on March 26.

By Saturday night in Breckenridge, the water was four feet deep on some of the streets. National Guard trucks were the only way to get around. More than a foot of heavy snow fell into the sodden town, and it was no improvement on the rain. It gave the streets the consistency of a Slurpee. Guttormson left her car on high ground in Breckenridge and hitched a ride to Wahpeton on one of the National Guard trucks. When she got back to Breckenridge on Monday, the car was frozen in place up to the bottom of the hubcaps. She had to pour hot water on the tires to get free.

The Red crested at about 19 feet 8 inches above the riverbed at Wahpeton, a record and one that rang alarm bells all the way down the river to Fargo, Grand Forks and Pembina. The high water would take about a week to wind its way along the 85 miles from Wahpeton to Fargo – about twice the as-the-crow-flies distance. Another week would take it to Grand Forks and yet another week would get it to the Canadian border.

Its heavy clay soil makes the Red River Valley highly prone to floods. Clay doesn't soak up much water, so 20 to 50 per cent of precipitation runs off the land into the river system. Compare that with western Manitoba, where runoff on sandier soils is 10 to 25 per cent.

The Red is also flood-prone because of its relatively shallow channel and the very slight gradient from its beginning in Breckenridge to its terminus at Lake Winnipeg, a stretch of 555 miles, a quarter of which winds through Manitoba. The Red is, in fact, flowing along the flat bottom of an ancient lake. Lake Agassiz formed when the glacier melted 11,500 years ago, and covered most of what is now Manitoba. Agassiz, named after a Swiss scientist who studied snow caps, was larger than all the Great Lakes combined.

The slight gradient – the Red descends only 25 feet from Emerson to Winnipeg – means the river runs slowly. So when spring runoff occurs, the river often isn't deep or swift enough to carry the water away. And when the Red's banks do flood, the water travels for miles and miles because the land is so flat – the highest elevation in the Red River Valley rarely exceeds 12 feet.

In Winnipeg, Warkentin went to work to find out precisely how much the situation had deteriorated.

"The funny thing was," he said later, "up to that point we were doing really well. We had had a lot of sunshine and temperatures around the freezing mark, and that made for a lot of evaporation." In fact, Warkentin was preparing to revise his March flood forecast down by three feet before the blizzard struck. Now the melted snow had been replaced and the region was in a deep freeze. Winnipeg recorded all-time lows – it was almost -8° F – on April 9 and 10. The water was piled high and pent up.

The blizzard presented a special challenge to Warkentin because it dispersed the snow haphazardly. "In a blizzard, calculations can easily be out 50 per cent," Warkentin said. "Environment Canada studies show that." Part of the problem is many precipitation gauges in the province have been automated in recent years, and they aren't as accurate as manual readings. But there are problems even with manual readings. "Where do you measure the snow after a blizzard?" Warkentin asked. "At the top of the drift? At the bottom? Or in between? And we had at least four significant blizzards last winter."

The accuracy is crucial. Small errors in snow water content can easily throw flood forecasts off by up to 100 per cent. So after the blizzard, the province wisely contracted the Airborne Gamma Radiation Snow Survey airplane, owned by the National Weather Service in the United States, to survey the Red River Valley.

The technology determines water content by reading radiation levels in soils. All soils contain trace radiation and moisture in or over the soil weakens the radiation readings. Fortunately for Warkentin, Environment Canada had mapped the soil moisture content the previous fall. Warkentin factored out the decrease in radiation that was attributable to the soil moisture. Further weakening of the readings would be the result of snow cover.

Whatever the findings, Warkentin knew his report would be bleak. There had already been a near-record amount of snow in the Red River basin. Around Wahpeton, there had been more than 100 inches of snow – about double the norm. Around Winnipeg, there had been about 65 inches. Across the whole valley, the average was about 84 inches. That wasn't a record; in 1956 there had been almost 100 inches

of snow. But a long, slow thaw spared Manitoba that spring.

The 1997 thaw had started out ideally, too, with warm days shrinking the snow cover markedly. But now all the gain had been cancelled, and then some, by the blizzard.

The gamma radiation readings showed the blizzard had dropped 19 inches of snow on Winnipeg. Across the Red River Valley, the radiation readings showed the equivalent of two to 3.5 inches of water had fallen on the wide, flat landscape.

That much water would raise the Red River by four feet. "It was a lot, because we were already predicting that river levels would be over bank levels," Warkentin said. His first April forecast was for a flood a foot higher than the 1979 monster.

The flood would be bigger than the celebrated flood of 1950. It would be a flood, Warkentin now knew, like no living Manitoban had seen.

Negotiating Portage Avenue (above).

Errol Funk (left) had to shovel his way out of his Winnipeg home.

Chapter Two
GRAND FORKS

JUST AFTER midnight on April 19, icy black water bubbled up from the sewers and into the streets of downtown Grand Forks, N.D. Nearly two weeks had passed since the blizzard. The sun's rays had strengthened, the massive snow blanket had begun to melt and the Red's tributaries – usually insignificant prairie streams like the Boix de Sioux, Sheyenne and Ottertail rivers – were torrents. The city of 52,000 – and the 9,000 people across the Red in East Grand Forks, Minn. – had been under siege for days and the river was mounting its final assault. Already, parts of Grand Forks, a favourite weekend getaway for thousands of Manitobans, were under water. But the levees protecting the business district had held.

Grand Forks had built them – prudently, it thought – to 52 feet above the bed of the river. The Northwest River Forecast Centre in Minneapolis, part of the National Weather Service, had six forecasters working three shifts around the clock to continually upgrade flood forecasts. It had recently raised its forecast to a 50-foot crest.

The forecast was hopelessly wrong.

The river had puzzled the forecasters before, in the days since the blizzard. In Wahpeton, the surprise had been a pleasant one – the forecasters had predicted a 20-foot crest, but the Red stopped at about 18 feet eight inches. In Fargo, 45 miles north, there had been panic. Fargo, a city of 74,000, had built its levees to 38.5 feet. That would be enough, its engineers thought, to allow a comfortable margin of free-board – two or three feet. But on Wednesday, April 9, the National Weather Service predicted a 40-foot crest for Fargo, to arrive by the weekend.

The same day, President Bill Clinton declared the Red River basin in Minnesota and North Dakota to be a disaster area. The day before, the flood had claimed its first victims.

Pam Wagner, tiny and three months pregnant, was driving home to Kent, Minn., from her restaurant job in Fargo. With her was her three-year-old daughter, Tori. It's about an hour's drive south from Fargo,

Darrell Nottestad helps his mother-in-law across the street in Grand Forks.

U.S. military (opposite page) surveys damage in downtown Grand Forks at dawn the morning after.

and Pam Wagner was nearly home – just three miles away – when she ran into trouble. She hit a torrent of water running over the road, and the car was washed into Whiskey Creek.

That should have been the end of it, but the mother found incredible strength. She got out the driver's-side window, grabbed Tori and made it to shore. In the distance, a farmhouse light glowed. Soaked to the skin in below-zero temperatures, Pam carried her daughter nearly a mile through a frozen, slushy field toward a farmyard light. Then, 200 yards from her friend Carol Krump's home, the creek again stood in her way.

Mother and daughter lay down to rest and never got back up.

A U.S. Coast Guard helicopter found their bodies the next afternoon after Ron Wagner found his wife's car in the creek.

'The forecast was hopelessly wrong'

President Bill Clinton, Grand Forks Mayor Pat Owens, at April 22 press conference.

As Clinton declared the disaster and Vice-President Al Gore made plans to fly to Fargo – he visited the city on Friday, April 11 – there was a frenzy of sandbagging. But when the crest rolled into Fargo, it was 35.5 feet, safely down the sides of the levees even without their sandbag crowns. The alarming forecast was blamed on a malfunctioning river flow monitor south of Fargo.

Grand Forks Mayor Pat Owens was cautiously optimistic as she awaited the Red. The high water would take about a week to make its way down from Fargo. On Tuesday, April 15, the National Weather Service predicted the crest would arrive on the coming weekend at 49 feet. That was a comfortable three feet below the top of Grand Forks' levees. Purely as a precaution, 400 people in East Grand Forks were asked – not ordered – to leave their homes at night and sleep at a high school or a seniors' home.

The next day, Wednesday, the forecasters raised the crest to 50 feet and said it would arrive next Tuesday, April 22. Owens, the mayor, wore a pager as she walked the city dikes and got quarter-hourly updates from her engineering staff. The water was coming up fast, and the 50-foot forecast looked far too rosy. On Thursday, April 17, the weather service conceded its previous forecasts had been woefully flawed. The prediction was now for 51.5 feet – a precarious six inches from the top of the levee – by the following night.

National Guardsmen make their way through East Grand Forks, Minn.

A massive ice jam (far right) lodged itself beneath a bridge in Grand Forks.

8

Paddling was the best option on Cottonwood Street in Grand Forks.

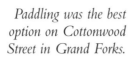

AP photo

AP photo

Trucks line up to dump their load on a dike as floodwaters continue to rise.

Volunteers scramble to fill sandbags.

AP photo

AP photo

U.S. Coast Guard rescue a man from his flooded home.

An elderly man awaits evacuation.

AP photo

9

A downtown office building (above) is engulfed in smoke and flames.
A Grand Forks firefighter (above right) and National Guardsman wade through downtown checking for fires.

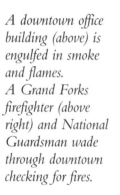

Smoke was still rising two days after a massive blaze destroyed Grand Forks' historic downtown.

The timing of the crest was spot on, but the prediction of the volume of water was no better than the ones that preceded it. In the end, the high water got to Grand Forks on Friday, but it reached 54 feet. There wasn't time to build the levees that high.

Still, Grand Forks tried. The April 17 forecast set off a ferocious round of dike building, but it was too little, too late. Mud and clay bulldozed into place on a frozen riverbank doesn't have the holding power of a permanent dike. When the bank thaws, the dike slumps down or is cut away from underneath.

In the Lincoln Drive neighbourhood of Grand Forks, the first dikes began to fail Thursday night at about 8. At 4 a.m. Friday, April 18, sirens sounded and the neighbourhood was ordered cleared.

About 1:30 p.m., the river topped dikes in East Grand Forks. Sirens wailed about 4 p.m. and a few minutes later, the Kennedy Bridge, last of the three that link Grand Forks and its smaller Minnesota neighbour, was closed.

Across the river, the Riverside Drive neighbourhood north of Lincoln Drive fell just before 5:30 p.m., despite hundreds of volunteers frantically sandbagging all day.

As the crisis deepened around 10 p.m., the city's emergency operations centre moved to the University of North Dakota from downtown. Radio stations abandoned regular programming to provide constant flood updates.

By midnight, the seemingly tireless army of sandbaggers was at the UND campus, bagging to blaring rock music as they worked to protect Smith Hall, a men's residence and cafeteria.

That dike held, but the ones guarding the city's downtown did not. In the early minutes of Saturday morning, following the bubbling in the sewers, the Red River came cascading into downtown Grand Forks.

It roared into basements, then into ground-floor shops. It sought out the electrical systems and shorted out the power. Great arcing flashes of electricity lit up the basements and found natural gas leaking from ruptured lines.

Within hours, the historic Security Building, an office building in the oldest part of Grand Forks, was in flames. Fire trucks couldn't help – the water was four feet deep in the streets. Standing in ice water above their waists, firefighters did what they could, but it wasn't much.

Helicopters dropped 2,000-gallon buckets of water into the flames. But the fire spread to 10 neighbouring buildings.

When the sun came up Sunday morning on the weary city, it found charred ruins jutting out of deep, cold water. It found 35,000 people homeless, taking refuge in strangers' homes, in school gymnasiums and

The remains of the Security Building, an office building in the oldest part of Grand Forks.
The flood shorted out its electrical system, starting a fire that spread to 10 neighbouring buildings.

Cattle were chest high in water at Randy Paulsrud's farm in Halstead, Minn.

Joe Bryksa

Joe Bryksa

Deer found themselves stranded on an ice floe near Oakland, N.D.

Dike building (right) continued throughout Grand Forks. Much of East Grand Forks, Minn., (far right) disappeared beneath the floodwaters.

AP photo

AP photo

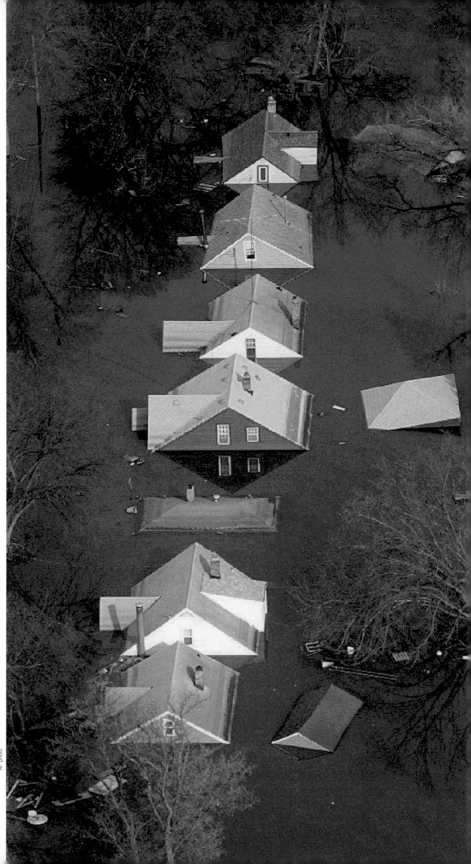

12

Jason Thorson, 15, left his home in East Grand Forks, Minn., for the first time by motorcycle.

in a vast hangar at the U.S. Air Force base west of the city.

Just over two hours' drive north, Gary Filmon turned on the TV set in his home on the Assiniboine River in Charleswood. Gary Albert Filmon, 54, was premier of Manitoba, a job he had held for nine years. He had been in politics for 22 years, first as a City of Winnipeg councillor and then as a member of the provincial legislative assembly.

Three times, Filmon had led his Progressive Conservative party to victory in Manitoba, to a minority government in 1988 and then to successive majorities in 1990 and 1995. In that way, he had matched the performance of his role model, former premier Duff Roblin. Filmon's popularity was such that, in the 1995 general election, the Conservatives had billed themselves as "the Filmon team" and kept the party name almost out of sight. Supporters and foes alike called Filmon a sure-footed political tactician. Both also called him a formidable adversary in debate, though his foes would have added that he could be downright nasty and personal. It was hard to remember that in his early years as party leader – he edged out establishment favourite Brian Ransom in 1983 – Filmon had constantly to stamp out caucus revolts and hear himself sneered at as "a wimp."

Before politics became his full-time job, he had owned a business school, but he was educated as an engineer – in hydrology, the physics of water behaviour, to be more precise. With all the province's information at his fingertips and the academic training to assimilate and understand it, Filmon was in a unique position to deal with the flood everyone knew was coming.

In fact, he had taken the weekend off to spend time with his wife Janice and their children. There were going to be some white knuckle days ahead and he wanted to be rested and on top of his game. He was cautiously confident that the province was ready.

Manitoba is no stranger to floods – much of the province is the bottom of ancient Lake Agassiz. The great, fertile stretch of land south of Winnipeg is fertile precisely because it is the Red River flood plain. The Red is Manitoba's Nile.

Filmon knew the province could expect water as high as it had seen in 1979, and perhaps worse. He had been out sandbagging earlier in the week – it was Volunteer Week in Manitoba – on Lord Avenue in south Winnipeg. The day had been pleasantly warm and that was promising. If enough snow would melt and run down the Red before the crest, a lot of suffering would be avoided.

"I kept hoping it wouldn't be as bad and I knew all sorts of things could conspire for that to happen," Filmon said. "One of them was that if we could get a lot of our water out of the way by having pretty good melting conditions, that maybe we would be better off."

"I kept hoping it wouldn't be as bad and I knew all sorts of things could conspire for that to happen."

GARY FILMON

*"scared
to death that
our information
was wrong."*

SUSAN THOMPSON

But a phone call broke into his Sunday rest. It was his aide, Bonnie Staples Lyon, telling him what had happened to Grand Forks. That's when Filmon turned on the TV set and knew "white knuckles" barely began to describe the month that lay ahead of him.

Susan Thompson switched on her TV that night when she got home to her condo in what used to be a fire hall in Crescentwood area of Winnipeg. Thompson was Winnipeg's mayor, a 49-year-old divorcee first elected in 1992 on a promise to freeze taxes. She hadn't delivered, but the electorate's consensus was that she had tried, and she was now in her second term.

She was Winnipeg's first woman mayor. Before politics, she was a buyer for Eaton's before taking over the family business, Birt Saddlery. Thompson's greatest strength and weakness were one and the same – her self-portrayal as an outsider. It got her ushered into city hall in 1992 as the new broom that would sweep away the bureaucratic cobwebs. But she feuded with administrators and civic politicians, and had a rocky relationship with the provincial government.

Like Filmon, she had had the flood danger near the top of her agenda for months. On the Saturday that Grand Forks flooded, she had been at a noon-hour briefing with Harold Clayton and the Emergency Management Organization.

Her first reaction when she switched on her TV that evening was that the same thing could happen to Winnipeg – she was "scared to death that our information was wrong." She tried to call Pat Owens in Grand Forks, but couldn't get through.

She vowed that she wouldn't be let down the way Owens had been. In meetings to come, "I think I was relentless, that's a polite word, in questioning everything I'd been given."

Winnipeg had resources other municipalities didn't – particularly engineers and a works and operations department that had expertise and experience with flooding.

Thompson had ordered one million sandbags in January, and in February the city had bought a second bag-filling machine. But the TV images told Thompson it might not be enough. When she got into her office at city hall on the Sunday after the Grand Forks debacle, she ordered another million bags.

The strategy for fighting a Red River flood is not to keep the river within its banks – that's beyond our resources. Instead, there are ring dikes around the nine towns in the flood plain and around the farmhouses and their outbuildings that dot the valley. And Winnipeg has a floodway, a 30-mile-long ditch to split the river in two and take half of it harmlessly around the city. A system of permanent dikes supplements the floodway and directs water into it. As well, there are two control

Firefighters (left) rescue one of 35 residents trapped in a Grand Forks seniors home. Grand Forks Air Force Base (below and bottom) became home for thousands of evacuees.

structures on the Red's principal tributary, the Assiniboine River. A dam at Shellmouth, near the Saskatchewan boundary, moderates the spring runoff, holding back much of the snowmelt from western Manitoba and eastern Saskatchewan and releasing it through the summer. And 62 miles west of Winnipeg, a broad ditch follows the route of the fur traders' 12.5-mile portage from the Assiniboine to Lake Manitoba. The route where the voyageurs carried their canoes lent its name to the nearby city where Harold Clayton had been a volunteer paramedic – Portage la Prairie. When the Assiniboine is high, water can be sent down the Portage Diversion to bypass Winnipeg.

Manitoba's dikes were built to the level of the 1979 flood – a flood that was nearly as high as the legendary 1950 flood, but did less damage because of the diking and ditching that had been done in the intervening years.

But the drowning of Grand Forks told Manitoba the dikes would have to be higher.

By the end of the week, in Emerson, on the U.S. border, 75 soldiers from the 610-member First Battalion, Princess Patricia's Canadian Light Infantry, were at work raising the ring dike by two feet.

The Calgary-based soldiers had driven the 745 miles to Canadian Forces Base Shilo from CFB Wainwright, where they had been preparing for live-fire exercises, after getting an order from Brig.-Gen. Bob Meating. In Shilo, the battalion commander, a lieutenant-colonel named Walter Semianiw, found a dozen soldiers with previous flood-fighting experience and used them to train the rest. The first 75 troops – Charlie Company – had finished training when the order came and they drove to Emerson to begin raising the dike.

Though they had come to help Manitoba – to save it, as things turned out – there was no welcoming parade. It was not a great time to be a soldier. Added to the hard work and poor pay was the burden of the Somalia affair – the death of a Somali at the hands of some undisciplined Canadian peacekeepers and the following televised inquiry.

For the thousands of enlisted men and field officers who would toil without rest for the next month – army, navy, air force and coast guard – the flood would cleanse them of the shame some of their commanders had earned.

It was a time for heroics because, in spite of Winnipeg's and the province's best efforts, the planning and preparations weren't complete. Among the myriad plans, something had been overlooked. Winnipeg had a gap in its defences, maybe a fatal one, and the Red would poke and probe until it found it.

Loren Reynolds, the City of Winnipeg's flood co-ordinator, watched the Grand Forks tragedy unfold on television from the city's Emergency Operation Centre. It was, he recalled later, "scary as hell. The adrenalin was flowing. It hit us – this is real, this is coming at us."

Reynolds, a former military commander, had established daily morning and afternoon meetings of the Emergency Preparedness and Co-ordination Committee. He thought the city's most dangerous enemy was complacency.

"I found it disturbing to hear people say that we wouldn't have a problem because our dikes are better," he said. There was a perception among the suffering Americans, too, that Winnipeg was smug and riding for a fall.

Late on the Saturday of Grand Forks' agony, Paul Wiecek, a *Free Press* reporter, trudged toward his four-wheel-drive truck to drive to a motel outside the flood zone and file his story for the next day's paper. He met a North Dakotan as weary as himself. Wiecek identified himself and struck up a conversation.

The Grand Forks man told him Winnipeg was complacent, foolishly complacent, behind its dikes and its floodway.

"Just you wait," he said. "Just you wait."

"Just you wait," he said. *"Just you wait."*

Bill and Lari Lampert were among those forced to leave their homes in Grand Forks on April 19.

AP photo

15

Chapter Three
DUFF'S DITCH

MANITOBA'S CONFIDENCE wasn't all cockiness and bluster. It was rooted deep in the province's history – a history of survival, of learning the tricks of the river and of making bold decisions.

One bold decision came early in the province's history. Just 14 years after displaced Scottish crofters established the community that was to become Winnipeg, the Red and Assiniboine rivers simultaneously rose up and washed the settlement of Red River away. The flood of 1826 has not yet been equalled. Even the flood of 1997 would fall short. It was a bold decision for the Selkirk settlers to move back to the junction of the Red and Assiniboine in the summer of 1826 when the water went down.

The river would threaten to wipe out Winnipeg again, most notably in 1852 and 1950. It was the 1950 flood, a disaster that forced 100,000 Winnipeggers out of their homes, that spawned the boldest decision. It was to build a system of ditches and dikes that would keep the city safe from the worst the Red could do. The decision was Duff Roblin's.

Charles Dufferin Roblin was a 33-year-old neophyte opposition member of the Manitoba legislative assembly in 1950. But through the 1950s, he won the leadership of the moribund Conservative party, breathed new life into it and led it in 1958 to the first of three successive election victories.

The Red in 1950 had flooded 10,500 homes. The property damage was calculated at $100 million, but that was in 1950 dollars. In Grand Forks, the Red flooded about 1,400 houses and damages were roughly estimated at $1 billion US, about $1.4 billion in Canadian dollars.

In the wake of the 1950 flood, two inquiries were called. The first, the federal Red River Basin Investigation, was established to analyse the flood hazard in the Winnipeg area. It published its nine-volume report in 1953, examining proposals for providing flood protection. It rejected higher dikes on the grounds that they would be positively dangerous if the water topped them, or in case of a major breach. Thus

Former premier Duff Roblin at the floodway gates in mid-April, as Winnipeg waited for the flood that had devastated Grand Forks.

Jeff DeBooy

The Red River (opposite page) is churned white as it squeezes through the gate structure at the floodway inlet.

A muddy St. Mary's Road in 1950, looking north toward the Main Street Bridge.

"It was called Roblin's Folly and, the name that stuck, Duff's Ditch."

DUFF ROBLIN

was Winnipeg spared the fate that would be Grand Forks's a half-century later.

The federal engineers said three proposals were worth pursuing. One was a retention basin at Ste. Agathe, to be formed by a 25-mile dike across the valley. Another was a diversion of the Assiniboine around Portage la Prairie and a 17-mile channel leading to Lake Manitoba. And third was a ditch around Winnipeg.

Engineers had long known the third option was technically feasible, but the common wisdom was that the cost would outweigh the benefits. But that supposition went out the window in 1950. That year's flood caused an estimated $114 million in total damages. A floodway was projected at $29 million to $82 million, depending on the depth.

The federal engineers weren't enthusiastic about the Ste. Agathe scheme, because it could not handle a flood much bigger than the

1950 one. The report's solution of choice was a Red River Floodway.

But the report gathered dust on the desk of Premier Douglas Campbell for the next three years. Campbell couldn't get a commitment from the federal government to help with the project. And in the 1950s, rural Manitoba held political sway over Winnipeg. There was little enthusiasm for a project that would tax the whole province for the benefit of the city.

But the Red rose high in the spring of 1956. Although there was no flood, there was a scare, and pressure mounted on Campbell to act. He responded with a Royal Commission on Flood Cost-Benefit. Its major recommendations: A 30-mile floodway around the east side of Greater Winnipeg; a dam and reservoir on the Assiniboine River near the Manitoba-Saskatchewan border; and a diversion channel from the Assiniboine River west of Portage la Prairie to Lake Manitoba.

The commission filed its report in 1958, just in time to drop it on the desk of the newly elected Roblin.

The benefits were obvious – a capital city immune even to a once-in-a-century flood would be a more inviting place to live, work and invest. But the cost was staggering. The Shellmouth Dam and reservoir would cost $11.5 million. The Portage Diversion would cost $17.5 million. And the centrepiece, a 30-mile floodway around Winnipeg and a system of dikes to make it work, would cost $63 million. The total would be well over $500 million in 1997 dollars.

The commission considered an alternative plan, improving the Red River channel below and through Winnipeg and eliminating a reef at Lister Rapids downstream from the city where preglacial limestone lies close to the surface. But this alternative approach was even more expensive, an estimated $123 million.

Roblin had won a minority government in 1958. On March 18, 1959, he tabled a government proposal for the construction of the floodway, and shortly after, managed to get his government defeated. The floodway would be part of the platform for his election campaign of 1959, and that election returned him with a majority. Now that he had the mandate to dig the ditch, it would take three years of planning and six years of construction.

Roblin is a courtly man and he will not name the prominent Winnipeggers who told him his scheme was a waste of money. But the project was ridiculed from the beginning. It was called Roblin's Folly and – the name that stuck – Duff's Ditch.

Duff's Ditch runs for 29.4 miles from the St. Norbert area in south Winnipeg to a point about a mile north of the town of Lockport north of the city. It goes from a minimum of about 24 feet deep near the inlet to a maximum of 67 feet as it passes through the hamlet of Birds Hill. The average depth along most of the channel is just under 35 feet. The drop is 18 feet from the inlet to the outlet – the same drop as in the natural riverbed.

The base width of the channel varies from 380 feet to 540 feet. At the top of the channel, it is about 700 to 1,000 feet from one lip to the other. A small channel at the bottom of the main one is up to four feet deep and 54 feet wide. There always is some water in that channel, except during extremely dry summers. The sides of the channel are sloped gently and seeded with grass.

At the inlet, there is a clay "plug." The 900-foot-long plug, which rises seven feet from the bottom of the floodway and is flat on top, is designed to hold back Red River ice so there is no possibility of an ice jam taking the floodway out of commission. The floodway gates are in the river itself, not in the floodway inlet. In 1965, engineers

Winnipeg Free Press Archives

Floodway gates at St. Norbert were constructed in the 1960s.

*The floodway —
pushed near its
record flow of
65,100 cubic feet
of water per second
— rejoins the Red
River north
of Winnipeg
on May 2.*

against the Red. The bottom flat side and the rounded rear facing downstream give the barrier side added strength.

If the gates were nestled into a hollow in a city street and then raised so the barrier side was vertical, they would stand 42 feet nine inches tall. But since they are never raised to 90 degrees, the maximum height they could reach is 34 feet nine inches. In practice, they had been raised to 25.8 feet in 1979, the worst flooding year Manitoba had seen since 1950. Like many records, it was to be broken in 1997.

Backed up by the gates, the river rises until its level reaches the entrance of the floodway channel. It is at this point, when the Red moves about 30,000 cubic feet of water per second, that the waters divide between the Red's riverbed and the floodway. To prevent scouring of the floodway banks, the channel was designed so floodwater travels at a velocity of five feet per second.

The floodway designers' calculations showed them early on that it is just about as important to control the outflow of water from the floodway into the river as it is to control floodwater entry into the channel. If water was allowed to plunge back into the natural riverbed at Lockport with full force, backwash and scouring could cause major damage. The designers built a so-called outlet alignment — a concrete rollway and stilling basin — to reduce the water's energy.

All that and more would be needed in 1997.

The final piece of the puzzle was a system of dikes to make sure the river had no way of bypassing the inlet structure and then spilling floodwater into the city from the west. On the east side of the river, the dike has been incorporated into the floodway itself with its elevated banks. To the west of the Red, the dike was extended about 22 miles to tie into a ridge.

It was more than adequate for a flood of the 1950 magnitude. It would not be until 1997, until it was almost too late to remedy, that engineers would find the dike was unequal to the task.

Expensive though it was, the flood control package brought with it an expected two-to-one ratio of benefits to costs. In other words, if it prevented a once-in-a-century flood, it would pay for itself twice over. As it turned out, the cost-benefit ratio was grossly understated. In 1979 and in 1997, Duff's Ditch was to stop floods as bad as 1950's and worse.

Roblin took his calculations to Ottawa and argued long and hard with the prime minister of the day, John Diefenbaker. In the end, the federal government put up $37 million, the province put up $26.2 million and the floodway went ahead.

On a rainy Oct. 6, 1962, Roblin and Walter Dinsdale, Manitoba's senior federal cabinet minister of the day, took the controls of a bull-

diverted the Red to the east and built the control structure into the dry bed.

The two so-called gates don't look like gates at all. If one were to take them out of the water and look at them from above, they would resemble two giant pieces of pie, rounded in the back, cut at an angle of about 45 degrees. If the gates were in fact pieces of pie, the pieces would each be 112.5 feet thick.

Put back into the river, right under the bridge housing them and the control booth overlooking the Red from several dozen feet above, the pie-slice-shaped gates lie in a hollow at the bottom, allowing the river to flow freely and boats to pass to and fro in normal summer water levels without obstruction or turbulence. During summer boating traffic, the submerged gates lie about six feet below the water surface on the Red River bottom.

In years when the Red rises beyond flood level and needs to be partially diverted, engineers activate a giant hydraulic system.

The pie slices, lying nestled in their hollows in the riverbed, now lever upward. Their rounded rear surfaces point toward the city and away from the oncoming water. The upper flat side becomes a barrier

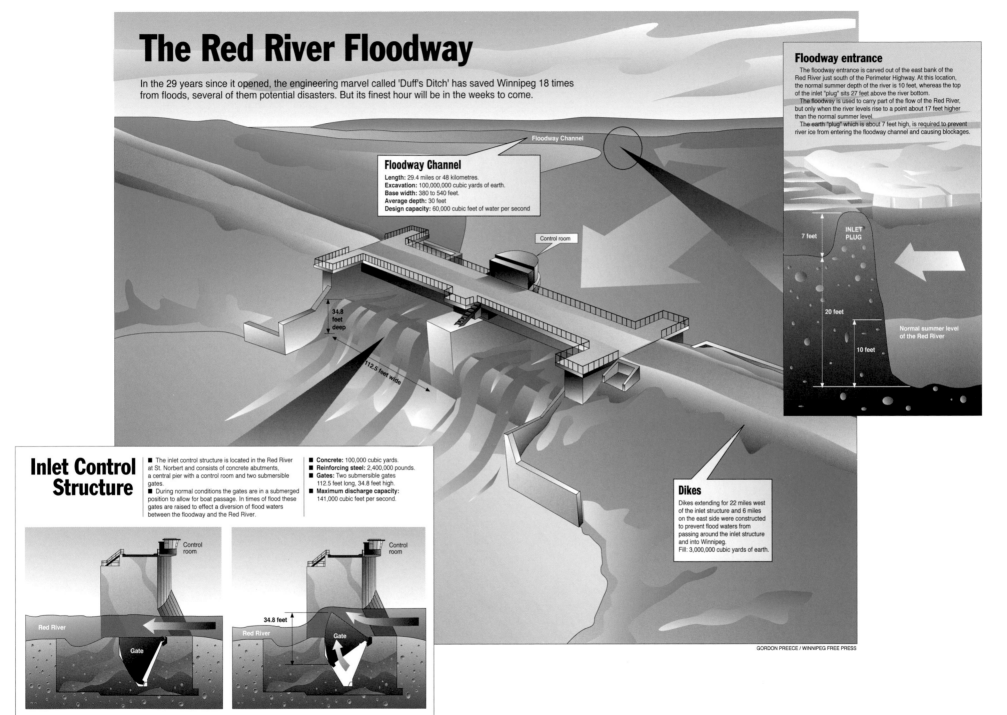

The Red River Floodway

In the 29 years since it opened, the engineering marvel called 'Duff's Ditch' has saved Winnipeg 18 times from floods, several of them potential disasters. But its finest hour will be in the weeks to come.

Floodway Channel

Length: 29.4 miles or 48 kilometres.
Excavation: 100,000,000 cubic yards of earth.
Base width: 380 to 540 feet.
Average depth: 30 feet
Design capacity: 60,000 cubic feet of water per second

Floodway Channel

Control room

34.8 feet deep

112.5 feet wide

Floodway entrance

The floodway entrance is carved out of the east bank of the Red River just south of the Perimeter Highway. At this location, the normal summer depth of the river is 10 feet, whereas the top of the inlet "plug" sits 27 feet above the river bottom.

The floodway is used to carry part of the flow of the Red River, but only when the river levels rise to a point about 17 feet higher than the normal summer level.

The earth "plug" which is about 7 feet high, is required to prevent river ice from entering the floodway channel and causing blockages.

7 feet

INLET PLUG

20 feet

10 feet

Normal summer level of the Red River

Inlet Control Structure

■ The inlet control structure is located in the Red River at St. Norbert and consists of concrete abutments, a central pier with a control room and two submersible gates.

■ During normal conditions the gates are in a submerged position to allow for boat passage. In times of flood these gates are raised to effect a diversion of flood waters between the floodway and the Red River.

■ **Concrete:** 100,000 cubic yards.
■ **Reinforcing steel:** 2,400,000 pounds.
■ **Gates:** Two submersible gates 112.5 feet long, 34.8 feet high.
■ **Maximum discharge capacity:** 141,000 cubic feet per second.

Control room

Red River

Gate

Control room

34.8 feet

Red River

Gate

Dikes

Dikes extending for 22 miles west of the inlet structure and 6 miles on the east side were constructed to prevent flood waters from passing around the inlet structure and into Winnipeg.
Fill: 3,000,000 cubic yards of earth.

GORDON PREECE / WINNIPEG FREE PRESS

21

Richard Beaudette surveys his property from the dike protecting his St. Jean Baptiste home.

dozer to turn the first sod.

When the ditch was finished almost six years to the day later, Roblin was gone from provincial politics. He had left to try for the leadership of the federal Conservatives and been beaten by Robert Stanfield. It was left to his successor as premier, Minnedosa undertaker Walter Weir, to turn the lever that raised the floodway gates for the first time.

That was strictly ceremony. It had been a dry spring and summer in 1968, and it was not until the spring of 1969 that the floodway was used in earnest. It was used again in 1970, 1971, 1972, 1974, 1975, 1976, 1978, 1979, 1982, 1983, 1986, 1987, 1989, 1992, 1995 and 1996.

The regular use of the floodway and the accompanying battle over the raising of the gates kept the ditch in the public eye. There was a debate every time the gates were raised about whether it was fair to push more water back on the Manitobans who lived just upstream from the inlet structure. But there was no such public stage for the dikes that ushered the overflowing Red into the floodway. They were built and virtually forgotten.

The inattention was to be nearly fatal to Winnipeg in the spring of 1997.

Up the valley, between Emerson and the south reaches of Winnipeg, people put their faith in experience and geography. The land along the river is so flat that when it floods, water spreads out for miles. There is no practical way of preventing a flood in the Red River Valley; the challenge is to deal with it when it comes. There is nowhere to divert the water, no affordable way to keep the river penned in its bed.

In his forecast after the April 5-6 blizzard, provincial hydrometeorologist Alf Warkentin predicted the Red would spread out into a lake that would be 25 miles across at its widest point. As formidable as it sounds, the dimensions of that sheet of water were the best hope for the farms and towns in the flood plain. It takes a lot more water to raise the level of a 25-mile-wide lake than of a 330-foot-wide river channel. Once the river overflowed its banks, the theory went, it would spread out more than it would rise, and all would be well.

At the beginning of April, Florent Beaudette, a farmer near the village of St. Jean Baptiste, was expecting something in the order of the 1979 flood. He'd followed reports as the Red began to crest at its source in Breckenridge, Minn. and at Fargo, where there had been some dike failures. He wasn't fazed. "What happens in Fargo doesn't mean all that much here," he said.

Beaudette, who has been reeve of the Rural Municipality of Montcalm for nine years, was confident until April 5. Then the stakes moved up.

"Then we got the blizzard and it changed the story," said Beaudette. "We were frantically looking for some number in water terms. When the number came in roughly three inches through the heart of the valley and two inches for 40 to 60 miles north, we figured we could well be in trouble.

"I don't think anybody panicked too much. We had a hard time believing once it got into the lake (spread across the valley) it would go to that kind of level."

Beaudette's family had farmed at St. Jean since great-grandfather Joseph Beaudette built a log cabin on the river in 1877, and had never been beaten by a flood. Florent's father, Edouard, had spent several rough weeks in 1950, surrounded by water and subsisting on Kellogg's Corn Flakes topped off with milk from the herd of dairy cattle he was tending. But that's the price you pay for farming the rich, black gumbo along the Red.

Florent had never diked his house before, but his wife insisted on it this year because they'd just spent $20,000 remodelling their kitchen.

Randy Turner

When the Red spilled over its banks on April 20, Beaudette watched it without undue fear.

And when his duties as reeve forced him to move into St. Jean Baptiste on April 21, lest a storm leave him isolated and unreachable, his brothers stayed on the farm to maintain the dike and Florent slept less easily than he had on the farm. "I'm more scared in town behind these high dikes than sitting at home with water lapping at the door," he said.

That same Monday night, Roblin threw a switch in the control structure where the floodway juts off from the Red. "It's nice to get this thing going again," he said. Everyone still called the floodway Duff's Ditch, but it had been a long time since anyone said it derisively.

Up the valley and west, in the hamlet of Riverside, near Rosenort, Rob Eidse was as confident as Beaudette.

"Then we got the blizzard and it changed the story."

FLORENT
BEAUDETTE

AP photo

A roadside sign (above) states the obvious on Hwy. 59 south of Winnipeg.

A farm truck (right) sits swamped and abandoned in the Morris-St. Jean Baptiste area.

Marc Gallant

The Morris River, most of the time, runs just beyond Eidse's back door. But when the Red runs high, the Morris runs backward. During the flood, the lake south of Winnipeg was sometimes called the Red Sea. By coincidence, maps of the north end of the flood zone and of the real Red Sea look remarkably similar. If the valley was the Red Sea, the Morris basin was the Gulf of Suez.

With the help of family, friends and volunteers, Eidse, a 42-year-old sometime construction worker and full-time photographer, started building his dike April 17, when Grand Forks was still convinced it could meet the challenge.

"No one around here thought it would be an issue," Eidse said. "No one was really doing anything. I got my dike built when I heard another guy up the road was getting a dike built. People said I was worrying too much."

But for Eidse, his home is everything. Like Flo Beaudette's farmstead, it's a slice of history. It's converted from the old local Riverside Co-Op store and it symbolizes his life's work and achievement.

The brick building looks like it's carved into the ground rather than sitting on top of it. That's because in the last major flood in 1979, the then-store owners piled dirt against the outside walls to keep water out. That embankment is still there providing protection.

"I'd been through other floods, like in 1979, and I knew because we were low I had to do something more to keep it dry," Eidse said. "And secondly, it's the only asset I have. I want to hang on to it so I can pass it on to my children. If the water got in, it would be history."

"We've grown to dislike water in general... But I'm not afraid of the river."

But like hundreds of people on their diked farms and hundreds more in the ring-diked towns and villages, he was sure it would not get in.

High water is part of the way of life in the farming communities of the valley – potentially lethal but at the same time, comfortably familiar.

Flo Beaudette has a long pole standing in his farmyard near St. Jean. Lines carved into it show the flood levels the Beaudettes have seen – 1885, 1950, 1979. Soon, Beaudette would whittle another line into the pole for 1997.

"We've grown to dislike water in general," Flo explained to *Free Press* reporter Randy Turner. "But I'm not afraid of the river. That's why I can live with it.

"Wet feet never killed anybody."

*Much to the relief of residents, the dikes around Emerson held
against the 25-mile lake the Red River had become.*

25

Chapter Four
THE VALLEY

HIGHWAY 75 was a double strand of dark grey ribbon across an endless field of light grey water. Along one of the strands – the northbound lanes near Morris – crept a convoy of 32 cars and trucks. It was Wednesday, April 23, and Manitoba's greatest evacuation since the flood of 1950 was under way.

Harold Clayton's Emergency Management Organization had ordered the virtual clearing of the Red River Valley from Emerson to Winnipeg. The sirens sounded at 5 a.m. Wednesday. In the next 39 hours, by 8 p.m. Thursday, 17,000 Manitobans left their homes. Already, 3,200 people in southern Manitoba had been ordered out. In Emerson, Letellier, Dominion City, St. Jean Baptiste, Morris, Ste. Agathe, Brunkild and St. Adolphe, only floodfighters stayed behind to maintain the dikes. And dotted across the sheet of grey water were the lonely ringed farms, each with a determined owner patching and piling his sandbagged walls.

For the past week, the bad news had been unrelenting. With the highest water, the crest, barely clear of Grand Forks, the Red was already out of its banks at Emerson by Sunday, April 20. It seemed no dikes could hold against the Red. Between Grand Forks and the border, it flooded Oslo, Minn. and the North Dakota towns of Warsaw and Minto.

Clayton's order to clear the valley came after a stormy meeting in EMO's conference room, borrowed from the provincial Justice Department, on the 12th floor of the Woodsworth Building. The room is about 45 feet by 15 feet, with a flecked blue, beige and purple carpet that took on the hue of coffee stains by the end of the crisis. Three tables were pulled together to make one about 30 feet long, with 20 phones. A clock on the wall showed local Central Daylight Saving Time, another showed Greenwich Mean Time. After the meetings, orders would go out from Clayton's war room adjacent to his office three floors up.

There were two meetings a day in the 12th-floor room – at 8 a.m.

and 8 p.m. That schedule continued, seven days a week, from April 18 to May 22. The cast varied, but there were usually about 20 people, representing provincial departments – Highways, Agriculture and Health almost always had representatives at the table – as well as liaison people from the City of Winnipeg and from federal organizations such as the RCMP, the Prairie Farm Rehabilitation Administration and National Defence.

The National Defence representative at the meeting on Tuesday, April 22, was a Calgary-based brigadier-general, Bob Meating. Meating was then the senior officer in Manitoba, at the head of about 1,000 soldiers who were the first response to the province's call for military aid. He arrived in Manitoba on April 18, just in time to see the coverage of the Grand Forks disaster.

Vic Braun (opposite) and his daughter Lisa took their pet owl with them, in a covered cage, when they left home in St. Adolphe on April 25.

A line of traffic was left with no place to go as floodwaters cut off Highway 75 outside of Morris.

Weary (above) volunteers get a tractor ride back to Winnipeg after sandbagging near Dominion City. The Roseau River (right) threatens the Pearse family farm.

Meating is a brusque man, and he showed little patience during his time in Manitoba for what he perceived to be civilian inefficiency and complacency.

"When I arrived in the province," he later recalled, "the press were very big on 'we are not like the States. We have our defences. We're ready. We're a hundred percent ready and we will deal with this.' And so I came in here believing, 'right, this is going to be a bigger flood than last year, but because they have the diking system and the flood-way, they have everything. The city of Winnipeg is going to be something that's manageable. We're OK; we have the floodway.' "

On Monday, April 21, he rolled out of Winnipeg's Kapyong Barracks at 5:30 a.m. to go to St. Adolphe south of the city to have breakfast and watch his soldiers fill and stack sandbags. The operation was planned to start at 7 a.m., but it didn't. The bag-filling machine was operated by a provincial employee, and he didn't start until 8 a.m.

To Meating, it showed a lack of concern. And he was disgusted to see that the roads from the south early in the morning were full of locals on their way to Winnipeg to work. He asked: "Who is preparing their homes, farms, properties for the event, potential event, of a life-time?" He decided that unless he took a strong line, the civilians were riding for a fall.

Here's how he described the rest of his eye-opening day: "I then got further down to Emerson that day. And I had been in an EMO meet-ing that day where I saw the volume of water (that) was dis-cussed. And I'm listening to people who have – who are the experts on it within the EMO – the people from MDH (Manitoba Department of Highways), the people from DNR (Department of Natural Resources) who have lived

through these things before. And they have been telling the people there that this is not a normal situation. And we should be ordering the evacuation or be taking more prudent action. I quickly realized there are two parts to the EMO organization. One is the agriculture people – agriculture and farms, animals and farms. And the other one is the highways and the resources people. And there is a conflict."

Meating would ally himself with the highways and resources offi-cials, the ones arguing for a quick and full evacuation. He would do battle with the agriculture officials, who generally sided with the rural residents who wanted to be left to tend and save their farms.

Farmer Robert Fillion refused to leave his home and land south of St. Jean Baptiste.

Some local farm machinery was kept high and dry along Hwy. 75.

Joe Bryksa

Joe Bryksa

Joe Bryksa

Marlys Pearse (far left) stayed dry when she and her husband Jerry left their farm near Dominion City.

Marc and Roland Gregoire, (above) near St. Jean Baptiste, kept an eye on their chickens.

The roof was the last resort for one man in Ritchot.

31

Rescue workers search desperately for 14-year-old Adam Young, who was pulled into an open culvert in north Winnipeg; his body was found weeks later.

> "I would move your animals and move your people while the moving's good."
>
> BOB MEATING

To the army, the operation along the Red River was warfare. In the alphabet-soup language that military people affect, it was an OOTW – an operation other than war. The command structure, the deployment of soldiers, the communications – all those elements were just like on the battlefield. When victory is the goal and the only acceptable outcome, you don't pinch pennies.

For its own political reasons, too, the armed forces could not afford anything short of success. The Somalia affair – a peacekeeping mission gone wrong, dead civilians, suspicion of a coverup and the unseemly evasiveness of the top generals on the inquiry witness stand – had given the forces a black eye.

For field commanders and rank-and-file soldiers, the flood crisis was an opportunity to wash the shame away. They succeeded brilliantly, but in mid-April, the army's redemption was yet to come.

Maj.-Gen. Bruce Jeffries, Meating's immediate superior, called from Ottawa on Monday, April 21. "Whatever you do," he told Meating, "err on the side of having too much. Don't worry about the dollars spent. Better to spend too much than not enough."

Meating's concern was to save lives. But the agriculture officials also had to be concerned with saving livelihoods. The clash of views would play out time and time again. Meating spoke out for the first time on Tuesday, April 22, at one of the twice-daily EMO meetings.

The topic was the hog operations that remained in the valley. Gus Wruck, the Department of Agriculture's rep on the task force, said, "You can't ask somebody with a $300,000 or $1-million operation to abandon his livelihood."

Meating thought the task force was putting dollars ahead of lives, that it was shrinking from the reality that was coming down the river, that it was fiddling while Rome burned. The general spoke up.

"I would plan for the worst," he told the committee. "I would err on the side of caution. And I would move your animals and move your people while the moving's good."

Meating had already been proved partially right – the water could kill. Pam Wagner, the Minnesota woman who died in the aftermath of the blizzard, had proved the power of the flood. There were three lives lost in Manitoba. On Sunday, April 20, Kevin Michael Maendel, four, had been swept to his death in a ditch near his home on a Hutterite colony near Portage la Prairie. And about the time Meating was seething at the April 22 task force meeting, 14-year-old Adam Young was pulled into an open culvert in the Maples area of Winnipeg. He, too, drowned. Later that night, a 40-year-old outdoorsman, Daniel Peter Leskiw, died in a kayaking accident on the swollen Souris River.

While the people of Emerson, Letellier and the other Manitoba river towns moved to safety – to the homes of friends and relatives outside the flood zone or into refugee reception centres in Altona and the St. Vital area of Winnipeg – the grim battle continued in the United States. In Drayton, the second-last North Dakota town before the Red reaches the border, officials bought two miles of plywood sheeting. While Meating was arguing in Winnipeg on Tuesday for a rapid evacuation of the valley, hundreds of volunteers in Drayton were nailing the plywood to two-by-fours sunk into the town's clay dike. Though a plywood wall won't hold back a flood, it will keep waves from breaking over the top of a dike and wearing it away. Drayton's dikes had started to leak at 3 a.m. Tuesday, and the governor of North Dakota ordered the town of 900 evacuated.

Drayton's only airplane runway was dug up so the leaks in the dikes could be repaired. "That was the only clay we could find. Everything else had already been used," Drayton Mayor Beverly Jensen said. "It wasn't much of an airport anyway."

As for the order to leave town, "I've been kind of busy, so I haven't actually received the governor's proclamation," Jensen said.

Drayton compromised for the next two days, with people sleeping outside the town but returning by day to fight the flood. Early in the week, the U.S. National Weather Service had predicted a 49-foot crest at Drayton – only two feet from the top of the plywood fence.

Earthen dikes kept floodwaters at bay outside Lowe Farm, about 20 kilometres west of Morris.

CP Photo

But on Thursday, April 24, the weather service revised its crest pre-diction – to 46 feet. For the first time since the flood crisis began, a forecast had been revised for the better. "There was a lot of us let out a scream and hoot and holler. Then we went back to work," said Tammy Puppe, who was helping reinforce sandbag dikes when the revised forecast came in.

When the crest reached Drayton later Thursday night, the dikes held. It was bracing news for Drayton's neighbouring town of Pembina, and for Emerson, just across the border from Pembina.

Sisters Kathy Wiebe and Helena Lefrance check out a flooded bridge on Hwy. 75 at the Morris dike.

Phil Hossack

Angelica Gehrer takes a close look at the erosion of a dike outside of LaSalle.

Marge Novotny, 69, is no stranger to flooding; the 1997 flood marked the third time the St. Germaine resident has had to leave her home since 1937.

In the rural Manitoba municipalities that touch on the flood zone – Macdonald, Ritchot, Morris, De Salaberry, Montcalm and Franklin – the reeves agreed with the decision to evacuate. They knew that if the high water came through the dikes, the people would be trapped in a torrent. But like Flo Beaudette, comfortable and confident on his isolated farm but nervous behind the St. Jean Baptiste ring dike, the reeves saw a fundamental difference between floodfighting on the farm and in town. Later that week, that point of view was to sharpen the confrontation between the reeves and EMO, where Meating's advice to clear the area was carrying the day. On Thursday, April 24, EMO decided to broaden its evacuation order. Now it would not be just the diked towns that had to be cleared, but all valley farms as well.

Early that evening, Beaudette and the other reeves had a telephone call from Premier Gary Filmon.

"It was a conference call," Clayton explained later in an interview with *Free Press* columnist Gordon Sinclair Jr. "It was a flood meeting, in the evening, 8 o'clock. And the premier attended with me and we had a conference link with the reeves as well as the flood committee.

"And because the premier was there, we connected to the reeves and mayors of all the impacted areas. Discussed the issue or possibilities of evacuation and it was just a general conversation to include them in what was going on here."

Sinclair asked: Was there talk about evacuation and the need for it?

"There was a talk at that time, as I recall, about the possibility of that occurring."

Was there resistance from some of the reeves?

"From some of them at the time, as I recall, there was, yeah. They didn't feel there should be a provincial evacuation order, that the municipalities were handling it."

Sinclair: Did he take a hard line on the evacuation? In that meeting, was his tone hard-line or was it conciliatory?

"No, it wasn't. I don't sense the premier took a hard line with them. That was left with our organization to manage. But he underscored the need – that there is a serious situation there.

"There were provisions to remain at their farmstead if they had an appropriate ring dike, they had an escape route, they had 21 days food supply for themselves and they had communication.

"That was worked out with Agriculture, along with the evacuation of animals and everything, long before this."

But it still stuck in Beaudette's craw that he was being ordered out.

About 10 p.m., Beaudette got another call – from an EMO staffer. There would be another conference call at 11. But when Beaudette called, the number he'd been given wasn't in service. EMO told him

South of Winnipeg, the "Red Sea" spread out
to submerge everything in its path.

Joe Bryksa

there was a problem with the line, that the call was already in progress, and that they'd call back with another number. When EMO called back, it was to tell Beaudette he'd missed the conference call, but somebody would be down to see him first thing in the morning.

Friday morning at 7 a.m., a Mountie pounded on the door of Beaudette's mother's house in St. Jean. That's where Beaudette had been sleeping since he'd been forced to leave the farm. A helicopter would be there shortly to take him to a meeting in Morris. In Morris, a Mountie stayed at his elbow wherever he went – even when he ducked out for a smoke. "Is this martial law?" one rural councillor asked.

Emerson was already an island. Morris, where they were meeting, would be cut off by the end of the week. So would St. Jean and Rosenort.

Over the phone, EMO told them there had been a meeting the day before with the army, and the entire valley was being evacuated south of Highway 205, farmers and all. The RCMP told them all the communities were going to go under – news to the people actually living in the communities, who knew how high the water was and how secure their dikes were. The RCMP said they would no longer stay in the ring-diked communities overnight.

...a fax that said "the area is no longer safe for anyone"

That Sunday, EMO issued orders to clear the valley south of Winnipeg, with a fax that said the "area is no longer safe for anyone." The army pulled out of Morris.

The reeves and their councils were still the authority, so the reeves were to sign the evacuation orders. They all said they wouldn't sign.

Beaudette could see the logic of evacuating the towns. Built low along the river and diked high, they would be death traps if the dikes broke. In Emerson, for example, the water against the dike was as high as the second-storey windows in town.

But it drove him and the other reeves nearly apoplectic that they could not seem to get the message across to EMO, the army and the Mounties that it was a different story on a farm. Most of the farmsteads were built on what passes for high ground in the valley, where an elevation of 12 feet is a mountain. Then they were ring-diked close to the buildings.

Darlene and John Santos returned to their home in the R.M. of Ritchot to retrieve a few possessions.

Outside the ring dike at Emerson, little survived the wrath of the Red.

Ken Gigliotti

The border crossing didn't stop the floodwaters at Emerson.

So if a farm flooded, the water would creep up and in, instead of roaring down on the floodfighters' heads. But nobody would listen to Beaudette. He was bitter about it then, and he's bitter now.

EMO, relying on the provincial declaration of emergency, overrode the local councils' authority. The RCMP made no arrests during the flood, but they arrived on farmers' doorsteps with the army and hand-cuffs and really gave them no choice – they could leave peacefully or in handcuffs. But most people who were forced out were back in their homes by the next evening.

Eventually, EMO gave up trying to force the evacuation of out-of-town homes. Clayton wrote a letter to the Mounties, advising them to use their best judgment, case by case. The handcuffs disappeared.

In Emerson on Thursday afternoon, April 24, RCMP Sgt. John Fleming ordered *Free Press* reporter Bruce Owen out of town.

Fleming had logic on his side. The crest of the Red was about to sub-merge Highway 75 and break Emerson's tenuous land link with the rest of Manitoba. Fleming said he appreciated the work Owen had done and the four-wheel-drive truck he had brought to town. But now it was time to pare the population of Emerson down in case there had to be a rescue by air or water.

"If the dike breaks, no one can tell me how long it will take for there to be eight feet of water everywhere in town," Fleming told Owen, his hand on the reporter's shoulder. "That's why I want you gone. But I want to thank you. You worked hard like everyone else, but now the dike is finished and it is time for you to go. If you don't go, I will arrest you."

Owen left. That weekend, he was in Rosenort, where he hitched a ride on an armed forces Zodiac boat. It skimmed past Rob Eidse's home in Riverside, and Owen hailed Eidse and his son Keith. Father and son were too weary from round-the-clock dike-watching to talk. Eidse just nodded.

They would fight the river for nearly four more weeks and they would save their home. They were luckier than many others. Already, a quarter of the 3,500 diked properties outside the towns had gone under.

By Saturday, the Red River was near its peak at Emerson, and it was 18 miles wide. "It's an awesome, awesome amount of water heading north," said Mayor Wayne Arseny, standing on the town dike, four feet above the water.

"Gawd, is it all going to fit in Duff's Ditch?"

In fact, it was the biggest river in North America. There was more water going north down the Red than south down the Mississippi; more water rolling past Emerson than past New Orleans. But Arseny had reason to be optimistic, even cheerful. The Red crested Sunday, April 27, at a fraction under 792.5 feet above sea level. The expected crest had been 795 feet. The dikes were built to 797. Emerson was still standing and it had 2.5 more feet of insurance than Arseny had expected.

There remained one great danger: wind. On a lake like the Red River had now become, a hard, steady wind will whip up waves that will chew through roads and dikes like they were made of sugar. Cruelly, just as the southernmost Manitobans celebrated the arrival of a lower-than-expected crest, the forecast was for high wind, wind that would blow up to 35 miles an hour across the miles of floodwater. It would churn the lake into whitecaps three feet high. The waves would rip and tear at dikes all the way from Emerson to Winnipeg.

And not all the dikes would hold.

Farmer Ed Zylema was swamped on St. Mary's Road.

No man was an island at Rosenort.

Zylema slogs through the floodwater with his valuables.

"It's an awesome, awesome amount of water heading north."

WAYNE ARSENY
Emerson Mayor

A solid ring dike – the combined effort of the military and dozens of volunteers – spared Emerson from the ravages of the flood. The two lines of trees show the normal channel of the river.

Ken Gigliotti

Wayne Glowacki

Marc Bruneau took to the water to check on his neighbours' diked homes in Grande Pointe.

Jeff DeBooy

AP photo

Floodwaters know no boundaries.

CP photo

David Bessason brought along an extra pair of boots to help sandbag a home outside Winnipeg.

Jeff DeBooy

Cpl. Don Leduc near Rosenort.

CP photo

Jeff DeBooy

The Desaulniers brothers hauled clothing and other essentials from a friend's home near Winnipeg.

Traffic was indeed slowed near Rosenort.

A group of friends and volunteers south of Winnipeg worked furiously to complete a ring dike and save a family's farm from ruin.

Ste. Agathe fell prey to the floodwaters within an hour when the village's dike failed early on April 29.

44

A canoe was left abandoned as traffic continued to move on Hwy. 59.

CP photo

A snowy knoll near a sandbagged house looks like a huge iceberg bearing down on the Titanic.

Seven-year-old Patrick Lansard (opposite page) checks out the scene from a sandbag dike outside Winnipeg.

CP photo

Jon Thordarson

A radio-equipped soldier (right) patrols dikes around a home on St. Mary's Road south of Winnipeg.

Irvin Dueck raises his dike (bottom right) using sandbags from homes that had been lost.

The military dubbed this home south of the floodway "Pump 15" as it took the work of 15 pumps to combat seepage.

48

Rick Friesen wades in to check the dike at a home near Rosenort.

Dr. Ernest Samuels hands a sandbag to his son Emile as efforts to shore up dikes near Marchand continue.

Ken Arnason, (opposite page) a member of the Coast Guard Auxiliary from Gimli, beaches his Zodiac on Hwy. 330.

Sandbags arrived by front end loader on St. Mary's Road south of Winnipeg.

51

The military
hauls a load
of sandbags
to shore up the
dike surrounding
Paul Guenette's
barn east of
Ile des Chenes.

Jeff DeBooy

No one at the Blue Clay Hutterite Colony was spared the back-breaking work involved with protecting the community near St. Jean Baptiste.

Chapter Five
THE DIKE

AS THE last week of April approached, the Red River Valley was a sheet of water. Waterworld, the armed forces people called it as they invaded it by boat, helicopter and 10-ton Heavy Logistic Vehicle, Wheeled – what civilians would call a truck. Waterworld was sparsely inhabited – a corporal's guard of floodfighters patrolled each of the eight ring-diked towns, and a scattering of stubborn farmers held out behind their sandbags.

Most of the 17,000 people who had left were able to move in with friends and relatives outside the flood zone. Others were processed through refugee centres in Altona and the Winnipeg suburb of St. Vital, and were lodged in hotels.

But the water was still coming up, and the news from upstream, from North Dakota and Minnesota, was nothing but bad. The Red was breaking through the defences of every city and town in its path. In Winnipeg, Morris, Letellier and Emerson, dog-tired floodfighters had to face the reality that all their toil, tears and sweat had merely been the skirmish before the battle – the high water was still to come.

April 24 brought the first ray of hope – the survival of Drayton, N.D. Then came the news that Pembina, N.D. had also withstood the crest, as did Emerson.

But few noticed the good news and fewer celebrated. Because, early on the morning of Monday, April 21, a Highways Department hydrology engineer, looking at a map of the floodwaters, had discovered Winnipeg's Achilles heel.

Ron Richardson, 40, short-statured, greying, had moved to the Highways Department from Natural Resources seven years before, figuring there was more chance for promotion.

He lives in Oak Bluff, where he coaches the 10-year-old Macdonald Mites girls baseball team that his daughter Robyn plays for.

It was only natural that Richardson would pay particular attention to the area around his home.

And that's how he saw that the projected flood area – dark blue on a map that Natural Resources had circulated – got too close to the La Salle River. In fact, the flood would go three miles into the La Salle watershed.

The implication was enormous. The La Salle is the Red's last tributary before the Assiniboine and it flows into the Red at La Barriere Park in St. Norbert. That's north of the floodway gate and behind Winnipeg's primary dike system. As many as 100,000 Winnipeggers would be forced from their homes if enough water got over the high ground and came down the La Salle or even the Assiniboine.

"And I wondered how it wouldn't make an end run and land in the La Salle basin – this way," Richardson said, tracing a flanking path around Brunkild, "thereby doing in Sanford, doing in La Salle." And then it would hit Winnipeg.

So about 10 a.m. Monday he called his old boss at Water Resources, Frank Barlishen. Barlishen's office is at 1577 Dublin Avenue, the same place where Alf Warkentin plies his trade. Barlishen is head of provincial waterways. He manages the maintenance of the province's 4,200 kilometres of drains that get rain and snowmelt off farmlands. Richardson had worked for Barlishen for six years and they kept in touch regularly.

*A military truck (left) plows through floodwaters on Hwy. 75
The 15-mile Brunkild Z-dike, (opposite page) designed to keep the Red out of the La Salle River, was constructed out of mud, sand and limestone at a furious pace; experts predicted high water was only 72 hours away.*

> *"...what keeps the water from breaking around to the north of Brunkild"*
>
> RON RICHARDSON
> Hydrology Engineer, Department of Highways

Ken Gigliotti

Joe Bryksa

Joe Bryksa

"So I just called him and, basically, off the cuff, asked: 'By the way, Frank, what keeps the water from breaking around to the north of Brunkild and dropping into the La Salle basin? Where's the end of the dike?' "

"Well, it ties into higher ground (toward Brunkild)," Barlishen said.

But the map kept tugging at Richardson's mind. His usual route to and from work took him past the floodway gates, and he often found himself looking at the massive dikes that shepherd floodwater up to the floodway entrance. He'd often wondered where they ran out. "Once you get down the highway, you just lose track of where the dikes are."

Richardson was still troubled an hour after his conversation with Barlishen, when Don Kuryk, the Highways Department's EMO rep, called a meeting in the office to brief staff on the flood. When that meeting ended about noon, Richardson edged into a conversation between Kuryk and Bob McKay, one of the Highways Department's senior engineers.

"And I just said: 'By the way, Bob, because you were out there for so many years, and you would remember the '79 flood, what kept it (the Red River) from jumping into the La Salle basin?'

"Bob was not sure. Neither was anybody else there. And I just left it at that."

The answer, though nobody could come up with it off-hand, was that the west dike was part of Provincial Road 305 and ended about three miles directly south of the tiny hamlet of Domain, about six miles south of La Salle.

"Later in the day," Richardson said, "I just – again, out of curiosity – I thought, `Well, I'm going to call Frank back and see.' "

Barlishen told him: "We're looking at it."

Luckily, he kept his word.

As Barlishen began to ask questions, Jon Stefanson, who had been the regional engineer in the RM of Macdonald back in 1979, recalled some water crossing over from the Morris River to the La Salle water-shed during that year's flood.

Steve Topping, the director of the Water Resources Branch, recalled later that: "All the oldtimers sat down and said, 'Yeah, that's exactly what did happen.' And they said, 'We need to look at this.' "

*An oil boom was used to break the waves
as work continued on the Z-dike.*

Late Tuesday afternoon, the call went out for an emergency meeting at 7 o'clock the next morning at the Highways Department.

After dinner Tuesday night, Richardson went for a drive around the Brunkild area with his seven-year-old son, Scott. Richardson didn't see him, but Frank Barlishen was out there, too.

Barlishen, with surveyor Hant Choy, was trying to do the same thing as Richardson: find out where they would actually tie in to the existing dike and extend it westward.

While he was exploring, Richardson saw that south of Brunkild, the Morris River was already flowing backwards. That meant floodwater from the Red was already running up the Morris channel. It would only be a matter of time, and not much time, before it found the low spot between the Morris and La Salle watersheds. When it did, the game would be up for Winnipeg.

Later, some questions would have to be answered. Should the gap have been seen sooner? By whom? But there was no time now for recriminations.

At 7 a.m. Wednesday, there were 20 people in a Highways Department boardroom on the 16th floor of 215 Garry Street, and they were stunned by what they heard from Kuryk. The dikes had been built to handle what the province called a PMF – a probable maximum flood that would occur once in 150 years. The flood coming from the south would be much bigger than that.

Among those around the table was Walter Saltzberg, 66, the Highways Department's director of bridges and structures. Saltzberg had been among the first to hear Richardson's concern about the dikes. It was a sombre and shocked group, Saltzberg recalled, who listened to the presentation from Kuryk and Barlishen.

"There was a feeling of disbelief. It was a feeling of – people almost were shocked... it was hard to believe the flood was going to be of the magnitude we were hearing."

The meeting was over by about 8 a.m.

If Winnipeg was to survive, the floodway's accompanying dikes had to be extended. But where?

"We had no idea of the exact elevations anywhere along that road," Richardson said.

A private survey company, Pollock & Wright, found the answer. It drove all the prospective routes at about 15 miles an hour in a truck with a receiving dish on the roof, bouncing a signal off a geostationary satellite. The dish let the surveyors take several elevations per second.

Richardson, Barlishen and a few others spent all day Wednesday looking for high ground and having Pollock & Wright map it.

Conventional surveying would have taken two weeks. But by the

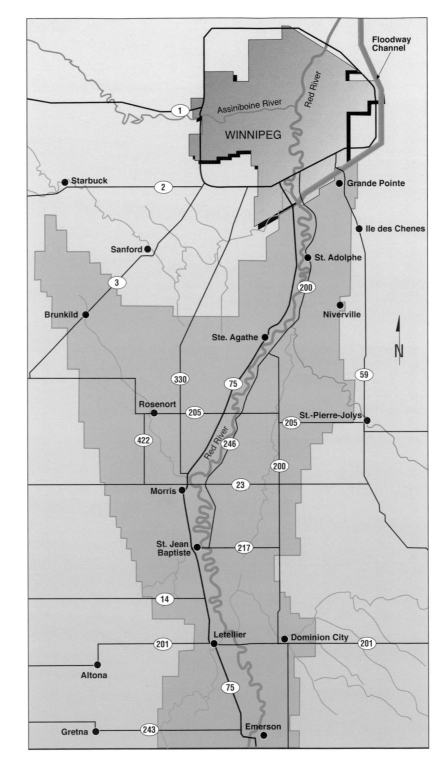

Map shows the size of the so-called 'Red Sea' during Manitoba's Flood of the Century.

Ken Gigliotti

Don Kuryk, the Highways Department's man in charge of building the dike, takes a good look at the work still ahead.

Jeff DeBooy

Flares lit up the night sky for workers on the dike.

58

end of Wednesday, the satellite had shown the optimum route.

It was a zig-zag, a Z shape, running west from the existing dike which started at the floodway and extended to the intersection of highways 305 and 330. The new dike started there and continued west, passing within two miles of the village of Brunkild, then turning north and west.

Warkentin's forecast said the high water was only 72 hours away from the Brunkild gap. The floodfighters had found Winnipeg's weak spot before the Red did. But it looked like they were too late.

They met again at 7 p.m. Wednesday, and it was there that it was formally decided the Z-dike would be built.

About a dozen people were there, mostly from the departments of Highways and Natural Resources. Brig.-Gen. Bob Meating and Col. Steve Appleton, from the army engineering unit, arrived later.

"The feeling was it was a very difficult task in the period of time that we had to do it in," Saltzberg recalled. "We chose the location of the new dike and we made some decisions as to what materials would be used where." And the existing dike would have to be built higher. "The initial assessment was we could build it all from the dike itself by using backhoes and just pulling materials back, except for some stretches of 305," said Saltzberg."

"Our feeling was we were facing a very major problem, for a number of reasons," Saltzberg said.

"One, how to get the equipment there in a hurry. Obviously, it wasn't there.

"Number two, would there be sufficient material in the dikes themselves to allow us to build them to the height which we wanted."

Third, how much equipment can work in one little area without interfering with each other?

Also, the ground presumably was still frozen. Not only would the frozen earth be difficult to excavate, it would be hard to compact sufficiently to stop the water. When it thawed, it would be loose and permeable. That had been the downfall of the Grand Forks dikes.

"So there were numerous concerns. I really think if we were not compelled – pumped up with the concern that we had to do it – you would not even consider that we would be able to accomplish it.

"I really think that a good number of people felt we will give it the Boy Scout try, but it is an impossible task. We were going to try it and we were going to put our best foot forward and do our best.

"But ..."

Kuryk drew the assignment of building the dike.

He called on private contractors, government departments and the armed forces. By Thursday morning, April 24, he had 30 pieces of

Some sections of the Brunkild dike were reinforced with 3,000-pound 'super bags' of sand.

Phil Hossack

heavy equipment at work. By Friday, he would have 300.

Farmers in the RM of Macdonald, whose fields would be cut in two by the dike, got short warning. But there were no complaints, no dickering over the level of compensation. Some of them lent equipment to the cause.

Three days was a ridiculously short time for a 15-mile dike.

To have a chance, they'd have to work 24 hours a day. But dike-building by the dim glow of headlights is slow work. The armed forces solved that problem. In the days ahead, there would be no night along the road from the floodway to Brunkild. Five hundred feet above the route, Griffin helicopters hovered with loads of 130-foot-long cylindrical phosphorous flares. Each one of them burned with a two-million-candlepower glow as it dropped by parachute. On the ground, in artificial daylight, work went on around the clock.

Kuryk used whatever material came to hand. Some sections of the dike were built of rich, black Red River Valley clay, clawed up from

Three days was a ridiculously short time for a 15-mile dike.

Cpl. Perle Coching monitors the airwaves as crews add to the Z-dike outside Sanford.

Workers lay plastic water barrier along the dike.

the farmers' fields by backhoes and packed as hard as iron by bulldozers. Other sections were of limestone fill, hauled in by the truckload from the quarries north of Winnipeg. The truck drivers found that if they inched their way along the dike, the ride was bone-rattling. But if they screwed up their courage and put their foot down, the shock absorbers would smooth out the ride as their 36-ton monsters took the bumps and potholes at 12 miles an hour. And some sections of the Z-dike were made of huge sandbags, 3,000-pound monsters that were dropped into place with a crane.

"I've been working so long I don't even know what day it is," one truck driver said as the dike rose. "It's got to the point now that when I go home, my wife says to the kids, 'That's your father over there. Go say hello to him while you've got the chance.'"

Originally, the dike was built with zero freeboard. That is, the forecast was for 785.5 feet above sea level, and that's the level Kuryk aimed to reach. If he could plug the gap, there'd be time to raise another two or three feet of freeboard so the waves weren't washing the top of the dike.

The job was a nightmare to co-ordinate. Only one truck at a time could haul fill onto the dike. And then the truck behind would have to wait while a bulldozer smoothed out the road ahead.

And on day two, it rained. Not a lot, but enough to make the clay as slippery as grease and slow down the rubber-tired earth-moving equipment.

'I've been working so long I don't even know what day it is'

Over in his office on Dublin Avenue, Alf Warkentin was feeling the strain. The demands on a river forecaster's time were without number. The railroads needed to know his latest forecasts to schedule – or not to schedule – trains through the flood zone. The Highways Department and RCMP needed to know which roads were going to be closed, and when.

Toiling away alone at night in the empty Water Resources building, Warkentin at one point worked 10 straight 16-hour days. There is a history of early-onset heart disease in Warkentin's family, and for the first time, he began contemplating his mortality.

"You start to think about your health. You wonder, 'Am I going to drop dead?' I thought about that a lot."

With wife Ursula and three children under the age of 10, that was not something Warkentin wanted to risk. But it was more than that. Should one morning find him dead on his office floor, who could take over?

Right, Premier Gary Filmon leaves by helicopter after touring the work in progress.

Old school buses (below) formed a makeshift breakwater on the Z-dike.

The answer was no one.

"Someone would try to do it, but they wouldn't have a clue. It would be impossible," Warkentin said. He was not boasting.

Papers and records and books and maps and manuscripts are scrolled up or on shelves or stacked against walls or lying flat on the floor in his office and rooms throughout the Water Resources building. To anyone but Warkentin, it looks like absolute mayhem.

It was a colossal oversight by the province to have so much riding on one man.

The gods smiled on the Brunkild dike builders. First, the network of roads between the Red River and the dike helped slow down the approach of the flood. And second, the wind came from the north. That made things dicier for towns like Morris, where water pushed up against the dikes on the north side of town, but it bought time for the Z-dike team by delaying the crest.

In the end, Kuryk had seven days, not the three he'd banked on, to work on the dike. And when the job was done, the armed forces gave him the Distinguished Service Medal.

The wind was a worry as well as a help. There was a 50-50 chance that it would blow from the south, and that would whip water up against the dike. When wind blows continuously in one direction over a body of water, it sets up wave action that will go through packed earth as if it were spun sugar.

CP photo

It was Andy Horosko, the deputy minister of highways, who came up with the idea of putting a breakwater out in front of the dike. It was an eight-mile stretch of derelict school buses and crushed cars. Later, the army added 27,400 feet of oil boom.

When the water reached the critical Brunkild gap on April 29, the Z-dike blocked the way. It barred it as well as such a hastily built structure could. But what if it didn't? What if multiple breaches opened an unbridgeable gap? What then would stop the water from crossing over into the La Salle or even into the Assiniboine?

The 15 miles of mud and sand and limestone were to be the focus of everyone's hopes and fears.

Jon Thordarson

Military troops (above) used Zodiacs to patrol the Z-dike for breaches. The "Brunkild Bunker" (left) was finished in time to meet the rapidly advancing Red. But would it hold?

Ken Dyck and a friend survey the situation from the 12-foot dike protecting Dyck's home between Brunkild and Domain.

Equipment operators worked in a race against the Red.

Chapter Six
THE ARMY

OPERATION ASSISTANCE, the armed forces' response to the Red River crisis, was the biggest peacetime military operation Canada has mounted. Not since the Korean War had so many soldiers, sailors and flyers congregated.

Just like the river they were fighting, the armed forces people trickled in at first and grew to become a mighty flood. In the beginning, the soldiers slipped quietly into Manitoba lest they upset an already nervous population. A month later, when the military had saved the day and won the hearts of thousands, people thronged Portage Avenue and Main Street to wave a tearful goodbye to their troops.

It was a love-in on the streets and dikes, between private citizen and private soldier. Higher up and behind office doors, it was a stormier relationship between the generals on one side and the politicians and civil servants on the other. At times, the clash of personalities and philosophies threatened to drive a fatal wedge into the top of the floodfighting effort.

The armed forces' involvement with the flood began shortly after the early April blizzard. The first skirmishers were about 300 Manitoba-based infantrymen and reservists who helped sandbag around Ste. Agathe and St. Adolphe in the second week of April. About the same time, on Friday, April 11 to be precise, two generals met at the Chateau Lacombe hotel in Edmonton.

One was Brig.-Gen. Robert Meating, the imposing, tough-talking commander of the First Canadian Mechanized Brigade Group. The other was Meating's boss, Maj.-Gen. Bruce Jeffries, a Winnipeg native who was the commander of land forces in Western Canada.

There had as yet been no call to come to the aid of the civil authority, but the blizzard on top of the near-record winter snowfall told Jeffries he should get ready. He decided to get some soldiers on their way to Manitoba. If the situation improved, they could be turned around and no harm would be done. If there was an emergency, acting now would save precious hours down the road.

Meating's immediate reaction unit was the First Battalion, Princess Patricia's Canadian Light Infantry. The PPCLI regiment has three battalions. 2PPCLI, based at Kapyong Barracks in Winnipeg, was keeping the peace in Bosnia. 3PPCLI was at its home base in Calgary and 1PPCLI was at CFB Wainwright, in Alberta, for live-fire training.

On Wednesday, April 16, Meating ordered 1PPCLI to move to Manitoba. Walter Semianiw, the lieutenant-colonel who commanded the battalion, put his first units on the road right away. By Friday, all 568 of his soldiers had made the road trip to CFB Shilo, a few miles east of Brandon. There they stopped and waited for orders that would send them back to Wainwright to fire their rifles, or on into the Red River Valley for the adventure of their lives.

The orders, on Monday, April 21, were to fight the flood. For Semianiw and his troops, the month ahead was to bear an uncanny resemblance to the kind of warfare they were trained to wage. "The Red River constituted a dangerous, powerful and somewhat unpredictable mobile threat that posed a high risk to both property and life," Semianiw wrote in an after-action report. "As such, the flood water substituted well for an 'enemy.'"

As soon as he got to Shilo, Semianiw searched through his troops for any who had floodfighting experience. He found 10 of them, including one who had helped build dikes in Dominion City in 1979. Semianiw asked them what equipment would be needed and turned them into his training cadre. For the two days after they got to Shilo, the battalion trained in the use of boats, rescue, dike-building and dike repair and a review of hazardous material threats. They reviewed first aid procedures for hypothermia, electrocution and near-drowning. They turned in their rifles to the quartermasters and drew, in their place, hip waders, rubber boots, waterproof combat gloves, immersion suits, heavy-duty flashlights and fluorescent vests and gloves for traffic control.

Convoy (above) heads down Portage Avenue.
An amphibious armoured personnel carrier (opposite) navigates the waters on its return to Winnipeg.

65

CP photo

Soldiers from Kingston, Ont. prepare for duty in Manitoba.

Phil Hossack

As the Patricias trained on Friday, Filmon and his cabinet put in their official request for military aid. The next day, Grand Forks was destroyed. The Red River was invading and it was time for the Patricias to go to war. At about 8 p.m. Monday, the 75 soldiers in 1PPCLI's Charlie Company had just finished their training when Semianiw got the call from Meating.

In a way, the battalion and the emergency were made for each other. Four rural municipalities – Montcalm, Franklin, De Salaberry and Morris – bore the brunt of the flood. As it happened, 1PPCLI broke down into four rifle companies. Company C for Charlie went to the RM of Franklin, raising the dike at Emerson. D Coy went to the RM of Montcalm, helping out in Letellier and St. Jean Baptiste; A Coy went to De Salaberry, where St. Pierre-Jolys was threatened by water backing up the Rat River from the Red. And E Coy went to Morris, which figured to be the most endangered town on the Red. So each of Semianiw's rifle companies had one and only one municipal government to deal with. Liaison with the civil authority was a problem solved.

Semianiw set up his headquarters in Altona. It was outside the flood zone, but close to the edge. It had Highway 30 and a paved airfield, it had a fully-equipped hospital and it had the regional EMO radio station. It would be 1PPCLI's home until May 17.

Just as though it was a shooting war, Semianiw did not try to micro-manage every detail. The situation changed too quickly for that. His company commanders knew his general intent and they had freedom of action, restricted only by an order that lives were not to be risked solely to save property.

In his summation, Semianiw said his troops had used all their combat training, all their combat vehicles and all their equipment except their weapons.

A military exercise of the size of Operation Assistance, even in the controlled conditions of a Canadian Forces base, is almost certain to mean some serious injuries. Deaths aren't uncommon. But even with the Red River doing a credible job of being the enemy – one that never slept as well as one that never shot back – there were no deaths among the floodfighters, military or civilian. Two soldiers were badly hurt, though.

Pte. Dan Rummery, a 23-year-old Winnipegger with the Edmonton-based 1 Combat Engineer Regiment, lost his right eye while changing a tire in early May. And Cpl. Frank Guay, 26, from the same regiment, was badly burned when his Zodiac inflatable boat ran into a live hydro wire near Emerson in late April. He later had to have his left hand amputated.

Maj.-Gen. Bruce Jeffries inspects the Emerson dike.

While Semianiw fought the river from Altona, Meating tilted with the city and provincial governments. The hottest and most public outburst came on the morning of Saturday, April 26. Soldiers and politicians were at the military terminal of 17 Wing, on the west side of Winnipeg International Airport, to greet and brief Prime Minister Jean Chretien.

Among the assembled cast were Filmon, Meating and David Iftody, the member of Parliament for Provencher riding. Iftody was the first of the three to arrive. He was in the terminal when Filmon, looking shaken and angry, came in. He had just witnessed a clash between one of his top aides, cabinet clerk Don Leitch, and Meating. The trigger was the confused line of authority at the Roseau River Indian Reserve.

"You know it's rarely that you see the premier upset," Iftody said later. "But he looked very visibly shaken and upset. And there was a bit of a confrontation in front of the media outside even before we went into the VIP room. And Meating was giving everyone hell and saying, 'Look, I want this Indian reserve evacuated.'

"The media had heard this. There was a little bit of a confrontation. Not with the premier; it was with — what's his spokesperson? — Leitch. Don Leitch. And Meating was standing in front of all the media people and saying, 'Look, I want those people out of there.'

"And Meating was saying, 'Why have you left the Roseau River Indian group in that community? They should be evacuated.' And then when the premier came into the VIP room, the discussion carried on between Meating and the premier about that. And the general was saying, 'Look, I want some answers to this.' "

Meating and Filmon had this in common: too many worries and too little sleep. What set Meating off was a report that a dike at Roseau had breached the night before. Meating knew the dike there had not been provincially inspected — that was a federal job. And he knew there had been nobody in the community mandated to give an order to evacuate. More politics. Meating resented the way politics dogged him at every step. Neither he nor EMO could give direct orders to the civilians in the valley's towns and farms; they had to go through the reeves of the municipalities along the river. And the reeves were stiff-backed men, not accustomed to jumping just because a provincial bureaucrat or a brigadier-general said so.

Members of Calgary's 1st Battalion Princess Patricia's Canadian Light Infantry fight 80 kilometre an hour winds while shoring up the dike at St. Jean Baptiste with logs and sandbags for breakwater protection.

Meating and Filmon had this in common: too many worries and too little sleep.

Ken Gigliotti

"I'm not interested in the politics of either one of you guys," he snapped. *"I'm interested in the lives of these people."*
BOB MEATING

Troops unloading sandbags at Lowe Farm.

Meating had been working 18 to 19 hours a day, and more often than not a phone call or his own worries interrupted his sleep in his little apartment at Kapyong Barracks.

What set Filmon off was being in the dark about any breach at Roseau. He should have been told. As it turned out, there had been no breach. The alarm had come from someone who saw seepage being pumped back over the dike, a normal part of maintenance. Meating had shot from the lip.

In the VIP room where they were to meet Chretien, Meating was belligerent with Iftody and Filmon. "I'm not interested in the politics of either one of you guys," he snapped. "I'm interested in the lives of these people."

Meating towered over the slightly built Filmon. But Filmon didn't give an inch.

He and Meating sat side by side on a couch and Meating spread a map of the valley on a coffee table. "And I also, I talked to him about the politics of the various communities up and down the river, too," the general said later. "About how people were staying in their ring-diked communities when it may be more prudent for them to reduce their numbers and to leave. That the emergency crews inside were very large, that I felt there was risk to the people that were inside. The ballooned numbers . . . And that they were putting themselves at risk but they were also putting potential rescuers at risk. So I raised that with the premier."

*The Canadian Mechanized Brigade of Edmonton was on the scene
to help Harry Waldner of La Salle repair his leaking dike.*

The Vandoos pull a Zodiac out of the water near Niverville as the storm gathers on April 29.

Politics was going to get somebody killed, he told the premier. There were too many people in the ring-diked communities, but the play of politics made it impossible to move them out. If a dike broke, some of them could die and so could some soldiers, trying to rescue them. And he – Meating – would take the blame.

The general and the premier recall their meeting differently in some ways. Meating, for example, remembers there being tears in Filmon's eyes. Filmon is certain there were not. But they agree on what Filmon said when Meating complained about being the goat if disaster struck. Filmon said Meating was wrong. "At the end of the day, general, you're not going to wear this," Filmon told Meating. "I am."

Meating had deeper concerns than the irritation of dealing with too many political levels. He hadn't voiced them to Filmon, but he had talked about them with Jeffries.

His responsibility was the area south of the city, but he was worried about Winnipeg, too. Its safety depended on the hastily built Z-dike. But, he told Jeffries, the city had no worst-case plan in place for the possibility – perhaps the probability – that the dike would burst.

Meating had met with Loren Reynolds, the city's works commissioner, earlier in the week, on Wednesday, April 23. The meeting was cordial and the men had much in common. Reynolds had been a military man for most of his adult life. He had been appointed commander of the Winnipeg Canadian Forces Base in 1986 and left the military to join the city hall staff in 1990 so he and his wife could stay put in a city they'd grown fond of.

But Meating thought the city wasn't being properly informed. Some of the city's information was 24 or 48 hours old. It looked to the general like EMO and the politicians were going to botch the operation and he would take the blame. It appeared to Meating that this was the first Reynolds had heard about the possibility, uncovered by Ron Richardson, that the water might outflank the floodway dikes, or the desperate discussions about extending the floodway dike to stop the water.

Jeffries arrived in Winnipeg late the next day, Thursday, April 24. On Friday, he, Meating, Harold Clayton and Hugh Eliasson, the deputy minister of government services, met in Eliasson's office. There were now about 3,000 armed forces personnel – soldiers and flyers – in the province. Jeffries pointed out that all of them were fully committed in the "lake" south of Winnipeg. There would be a need for at least as many more soldiers, Jeffries persuaded Eliasson, if the Z-dike were to fail. That afternoon, the province put in the call for 4,500 more military personnel. The immediate reaction unit from Central Canada moved to Manitoba, led by Brig.-Gen. Rick Hillier. The Royal

Soldiers and police boat from house to house delivering evacuation notices along Hwy. 59 on April 26; most residents refused to leave.

Marc Gallant

Pte. Peter Chan (left) of the Princess Patricia's Canadian Light Infantry hoists sandbags in Emerson. Warren Magnusson of the Coast Guard (above) on a barge outside the Morris dike.

73

Doug Nairne, reporter and reservist, surveys the situation in Halbstadt with a local resident.

"At times, there were people literally lined up outside our improvised barracks with homemade soup..."

Canadian Regiment and the Royal 22nd Regiment, the celebrated Van Doos, supplied the biggest numbers. Jet Ranger helicopters from the flying school in Portage la Prairie and Sea King helicopters from Nova Scotia flew in to bolster the Griffins and Labradors already toiling in and over the valley.

The arrival of a second brigade group and its commanding brigadier-general meant it was time for Jeffries to move to Winnipeg and take command of the situation both in and south of Winnipeg. At the height of the flood crisis, he would have nearly 8,500 soldiers, sailors and flyers under his command. His arrival meant that, for the first time, there would be a shock absorber between the civilian authorities and the abrasive Meating.

Among the first soldiers on the job and among the last to be relieved were the reserves, part-time civilian soldiers. They moved from crisis to crisis over four weeks, up and down both sides of the Red River from the American border to the Perimeter Highway around

Winnipeg, first building the dikes, then maintaining them, and finally tearing them down. It was back-breaking, painful work, spread out over 18-hour days and seven-day work weeks.

It was also, said Free Press reporter Doug Nairne, who spent the flood crisis working as a captain in the reserves, the opportunity of a lifetime.

"It was hard to go anywhere," he wrote later, "without getting a firm handshake and heartfelt thank-you from people who would cross the street just to be close to a soldier. At times, there were people literally lined up outside our improvised barracks with homemade soup, baking, farmer's sausage and anything else we could ask for. We received letters from school children, visits from church groups and more invitations to visit than we could accept.

"People offered us their homes to live in and their schools to shower in. They asked if they could do our laundry and made us feel like their lifelong friends and neighbours. Which, in a sense, we now are."

Soldiers were integral to dike-building efforts across the province.

Bdr. John Horan of the 1st Regiment Royal Canadian Artillery was among the soldiers who called La Salle School home during the flood.

It was the same for soldiers in the regular army.

When Cpl. Quinton Hooker got to Winnipeg from Edmonton on April 23 with 1 Service Battalion, he was moved by the crayon drawings from a Grade 1 class that decorated the walls at Kapyong Barracks.

"After a three-day road move, the next morning I was so tired, but when I got up and saw the pictures, I don't know how to describe the feeling. It was a feeling of warmth like being with my own kids," Hooker said. So he went to Ralph Maybank School to express his appreciation in person.

"My kids made some beautiful posters thanking all the military," said teacher Cora Campbell. "Cpl. Hooker phoned and wanted to come down and thank the class personally. That thrilled the kids to no end."

Hooker said the letter of thanks he got from the first-graders after his visit is his most prized memory of fighting the flood of '97, and he planned to keep writing the class even after his regiment left for Bosnia in late July.

At the other end of the chain of command, Jeffries felt the same warmth. Up to 1997, the most excitement Jeffries had seen was in Bosnia, in 1996, where he commanded a multinational UN force keeping the fragile Dayton peace accord in effect.

"It was a career experience for me," he said. "And then to turn around and do this (lead Operation Assistance) less than a year later. With more soldiers involved. With an emergency of epic proportions. For Canada, a natural disaster on the verge of happening and impacting on a major Canadian population centre. To be put into that position of responsibility, I think even the Bosnia experience now slips into second place. And then the reaction of the citizens of Manitoba to our involvement made it much more gratifying."

"It's not so much we were surprised by it," said Cpl. Shayne Demeria of the Royal Canadian Regiment. "It's just that we weren't expecting so much of it and the number of people offering thanks."

"We need this at the moment," said Master Cpl. David Wilkinson, from the same regiment. "We've had a lot of bad publicity. We're not used to this." What they weren't used to was children clambering on their equipment, families bringing their kids to meet soldiers, young women offering their phone numbers.

It was exactly what Canada's military needed, said military historian David Bercuson. "They're getting a chance to show they're not all a bunch of murdering bastards who kill people in Somalia or who shred paper at the Department of Defence headquarters," he said.

By the last week of April, the Red was so high, it was backing up the Assiniboine and Seine rivers. In apartment blocks along Roslyn

Soldiers battle against nature as wind and water turned clay dikes at St. Jean Baptiste into mud pits.

Soldiers load boats off the floodway embankment with sandbags destined for threatened communities south of Winnipeg.

Jeff DeBooy

The Kenny family credits the military for saving their St. Mary's Road home from ruin; the land has belonged to the family since 1879.

Road and Wellington Crescent, water pushed through the sandbags and poured into the basements. That made the buildings unlivable because it knocked out the electrical system, stopping the elevators and, more importantly, the air exchange systems.

The city prepared evacuation notices to 10,000 homes, every residence on the banks of any of Winnipeg's three rivers – the Red, Assiniboine and Seine. These were not orders to clear out, such as went to St. Norbert and Kingston Crescent. They were written notices to be ready to leave on 24 hours notice. Meating kept arguing for preparations to go far beyond a riverside evacuation. And when it seemed to him the civilians weren't catching on to how dangerous the situation had become, he made some moves on his own.

He asked for the immediate response units in Ontario and Quebec to be committed, to be ready to fly out on short notice. He asked for medical assistance and doctors, though not the mobile field hospital that headquarters sent.

He told everyone who came out to bring a life preserver.

He ordered up mobile water purification units, though not out of concern for the city's water, which comes by aqueduct from distant Shoal Lake. It was for people in southern Manitoba, which Clayton thought might be in the same fix as Grand Forks, or the Ancient Mariner of poetic fame – water everywhere, but none of it fit to drink.

"I just don't believe the amount of responsibility that I face here," Meating said. "It wasn't until the forecast of bad weather came along that I really think the people ... really took seriously the threat."

After his Friday, April 25 conference with Eliasson and Meating, Jeffries flew on to Edmonton with a copy of an operational plan written by another general – former Free Press publisher Richard Malone. Malone, then a brigadier-general, had written it in 1950, but time had not lessened its impact on Jeffries. The Canadian Army's overall operation was known as Red Ramp, but within it was a plan, written by a committee led by Malone and code-named Operation Blackboy, for the emergency evacuation of Winnipeg. It was time, Meating had impressed upon Jeffries, for the city to update Blackboy.

The city's state of preparedness turned out not as bad as Meating and Jeffries had feared. Filmon pointed out to Jeffries that there was a huge difference between 1950 and now – Duff's Ditch. Even the worst case would not mean clearing out all of Winnipeg. As well, there had been no Emergency Management Organization or civil defence operation in 1950. In fact, creating civil defence organizations across Canada was the major recommendation in the army's after-action report on the 1950 flood.

Troops travelled the province (left) to aid in the flood effort.

Cpl. Ed Capulong (bottom) steers a boat loaded with sandbags past a washed-out military truck near Ste. Agathe.

A military doctor arrives by helicopter to tend to a civilian truck driver working on the Brunkild Dike who had been struck with appendicitis.

While many houses in Grande Pointe succumbed to the floodwater, troops continued to shore up dikes for other homes to withstand the water.

Engine trouble had this member of the Royal 22nd Regiment, the Van Doos, temporarily grounded near Niverville.

CP Photo

Troops had their hands full sandbagging the ring dike that saved the town of Emerson.

Spr. Matthew VanErp does his best to keep dogs from the Roseau River First Nation from hitching a ride in his Zodiac.

Marc Gallant

And the city did have a planning framework, with its responsibilities spelled out in the province's emergency plan. One of Meating's staff had told him there was no plan, Meating said, and that's what he had believed. Later, he had to admit there had been some excellent planning. The medical plan, for example, was detailed in its timetable for which hospital wards would be emptied in what order, and where the patients would go. What was missing was co-ordinated detailed planning, and he was concerned about the ability of the city and the province to put all the pieces of their plans together, in a hurry, if an emergency struck.

Jeffries came back to Winnipeg on Sunday, April 27, to take up command for the duration of the crisis. The weather forecast was about as bad as it could be – high winds that would churn up dike-destroying waves on the lake that the Red had formed.

It was a sombre group of city, provincial and military people who met the next evening at 8 p.m. in a conference room in the Woodsworth Building. Among those present were Clayton, Eliasson, Leitch, chief city commissioner Rick Frost and the three generals – Jeffries in overall command, Meating in charge of the effort south of Winnipeg and the newly arrived Rick Hillier in charge of military operations inside Winnipeg.

First on the agenda was the province's plan for dealing with a major breach in the Brunkild dike. Such a breach seemed likely, even probable, with the storm forecast.

The province had hired an engineering firm to draft the contingency plan, and the engineers took the floor for the next 40 minutes. Their idea was to use helicopters to lift car hulks and school buses – the derelicts that made up the breakwater that deputy highways minister Andy Horosko had devised – and drop them into the gap in the dike. Then they would be shored up with truckloads of limestone and giant sandbags.

Jeffries, ever the diplomat, pointed out the flaw in the proposal – there weren't enough heavy helicopters to do the job. There aren't, Bob Meating thought to himself, enough heavy helicopters in the world to carry out that scheme.

"It was my impression that you couldn't depend upon that plan," Jeffries said later. "It was, in my view, not a practical plan." Meating, in his blunt manner, recalled the presentation this way: "It's a waste of money. I mean, I've never heard more – anyway, I'm not an engineer. But I understand time and space and people and getting your ducks all lined up to make sure you've got the stuff in the right place at the right time.

"The plan to close a hole in the Brunkild dike was so far-fetched it

Jeff DeBooy

wasn't worth the money the province paid the contracting engineer."

But at the Monday conference, Meating kept quiet and let Jeffries explain, politely and patiently, that the plan was a non-starter.

"Once I made that point," Jeffries said later, "then the whole thrust of the conversation turned to how, then, should we prepare the city of Winnipeg to deal with that kind of scenario. That's when we decided that a plan for a mass evacuation was a prudent thing to do. And I offered – in fact, I had foreseen that requirement – and I had Rick Hillier stand up and give them a thumbnail sketch of the kinds of considerations that needed to be embedded in that kind of plan."

Jeffries offered his staff to help draft a new Blackboy plan. He felt he had to tread carefully with the civil servants. Meating's bulldozer approach to disagreements gave provincial politicians and bureaucrats the fear that they were going to be elbowed aside. "And I understood that," Jeffries said later. "So my game plan was to offer them assistance in a non-threatening way at every step to ensure that they understood that they were maintaining control of this process."

The provincial and city officials asked for time to talk it over. They excused themselves and went to another office, leaving the generals behind. Half an hour later, as the generals had hoped, the civil servants returned. They agreed with Jeffries that it was time to draw up a single master plan for the worst.

Residents of St. Norbert, just south of Winnipeg, had to evacuate their homes quickly as the Red advanced.

Military vehicles became a familiar sight in Winnipeg (right).

Kristine Enns and daughter Katarina (below) make their way past a convoy on a city street as a soldier directs traffic.

Soldiers from 2nd Combat Engineer Regiment in Petawawa, Ont., entertain students from Glenelm School.

Jeffries offered working space at 17 Wing, and the evacuation committee met there at 8 a.m. Tuesday – oh eight hundred, in Meating's parlance. The meeting went on, for some of the participants, to 4 a.m. Wednesday. It picked up again at 9 a.m.

And a ray of sunlight appeared.

"During the course of the first day," said Jeffries, "the engineers continued to do their number-crunching. By the end of the first day, it was clear the flood forecast was nowhere near as severe as was believed on the evening of the 28th." At Morris, the water had been two feet lower than feared.

More number-crunching persuaded the city that a breach, even a major one, of the Z-dike would not mean catastrophe. As fast as the water would flow, there would still be time to push more water into the floodway to compensate.

The city, which had put 10,000 households on notice to be ready for evacuation, cancelled the warnings.

But the generals and the bureaucrats continued their work, to Meating's delight. He found civilians on his own wavelength, particularly the provincial Highways Department's Don Kuryk, who would get a medal for his work on the Brunkild dike, and Rick Frost, the chief city commissioner. Frost proposed going ahead with a plan to evacuate up to 100,000 Winnipeggers, not because the threat was imminent, but to have "in our hip pocket."

It never became necessary to implement the plan. The Brunkild dike held out and the crest of the river arrived at slightly less than the forecast level. For the first time since the blizzard struck nearly a month before, the river had begun to let up.

With the arrival of Hillier and the second wave of soldiers, Winnipeg got to know the military the way their neighbours up the valley had done earlier. "When the military came in, they became part of our staff," said Loren Reynolds, the city's works commissioner. "They were great.... Hillier was a real class act. I would say the military saved 120 to 150 houses, and that's a conservative guess." Mayor Susan Thompson wanted a military parade, to let Winnipeggers shower the soldiers with their affection and gratitude. Jeffries declined. Wary of disturbing the working relationship he'd been able to establish, he protested that the military personnel were not the only heroes – that all manner of people had gone above and beyond the call.

Brittany Martens and her mom (left) were among those who came out to a dinner in Altona for troops and evacuees.

Agatha Andres of Altona (below) had a hug for Pte. Kevin Dunne of Calgary.

89

A bit of rain wasn't enough to stop thousands of Manitobans from turning out for a parade to thank the military for its contribution to the flood effort.

Osborne Street in Winnipeg (left) was jammed with grateful residents when the military convoy passed on its way out of the city for the last time. Five-year-old Vann Hansell (above) gives a salute to passing soldiers from dad Darryl's shoulders.

In the end, Jeffries and Thompson compromised. A convoy of 130 amphibious vehicles, trucks and jeeps was to leave the city May 14. So that Winnipeg and the armed forces could salute each other, the convoy formed up at the Winnipeg Canoe Club on Dunkirk Drive, rolled up Osborne Street to Portage Avenue, down Portage to Main and then on to the CP Rail yards at Keewatin Street and Selkirk Avenue, where the vehicles were loaded onto trains.

Under a chilly drizzle, 15,000 people lined the route, waving flags.

It was a show of pride and respect that Canadian soldiers had not seen for years, certainly not since Somalia.

Jeffries said fighting the flood gave his troops a shot of morale, the likes of which he had never seen.

"I think it has helped the Canadian Armed Forces turn the page for

our forces," he said.

"I think they'll go home the better for this," agreed Hillier.

Guay, the combat engineer who lost his hand in the accident near Emerson, led the Red River Exhibition parade on June 22. Rummery, the other injured combat engineer, was invited to share the honour. Rummery, who was in Winnipeg the day before the parade to be fitted for a prosthetic eye, said he appreciated the good wishes, but he preferred to heal in private.

Guay said it was strange to be leading the parade. "I'm more used to being behind – in a mass of green," he said.

Both Guay and Rummery expected their military careers to be over. Rummery got a job offer from a Winnipeg engineering firm and planned to take it up in the fall of 1997. Guay said his injuries sometimes left him feeling "dependent and useless."

But self-pity isn't in Guay's character. Free Press reporter Paul Samyn dropped into his hospital room in Edmonton on May 7, 10 days after the accident. "Even when you go into combat, you don't think about things like injuries," said Guay, who had done 30 months of peacekeeping in Croatia. "Otherwise you wouldn't be able to do your job. But I had some bad luck."

Samyn asked if there would be a medal or some other sort of honour. Guay pointed to the greeting cards, mostly from Manitobans he'd never met, lining his room.

"This is pretty much my citation," he said.

Cpl. Frank Guay, of the 1st Combat Engineer Regiment in Edmonton, had his badly burned left hand amputated after his Zodiac boat ran into a live hydro wire near Emerson.

Chapter Seven
THE CITY

IN THE battle against the flood of '97, the great prize was the city of Winnipeg. It was by far the biggest community along the Red River, with a population nearly eight times the 80,000 people in Fargo, N.D., the next largest city. By April 20, the flood had Grand Forks and East Grand Forks, with a combined population of 50,000, under its belt. That victory solidified its claim to being the flood of the century. But if Winnipeg couldn't hold it back, the flood would establish itself as one of the greatest North American disasters in history.

There were those who thought Winnipeg would become the biggest scalp on the Red River's belt. In Grand Forks, late on the day his home town succumbed to the flood, an anguished flood refugee said Winnipeggers were foolishly complacent, that they didn't know what was coming at them. A few days later, Bob Meating, the often-acerbic brigadier-general who had come to Manitoba to lead the military flood battle in the Red River Valley, thought the city was ill-prepared because it was out of the information loop.

Both men were wrong. Of all the communities, large and small, along the Red, Winnipeg was uniquely prepared to deal with the flood, and not just because it was guarded by the Red River Floodway. It had engineers who were familiar with dikes and hydraulics, it had a works department familiar with dike construction and it had a mechanism for dealing with emergencies and co-ordinating its emergency operations with those of the province.

Loren Reynolds, a former military officer in Air Command who was now the civic parks and protection commissioner, took on the job of chief city floodfighter. Reynolds had an emergency preparedness committee that met twice daily. After the flood, Reynolds gave that committee much of the credit for Winnipeg's escape. "There was a cadre of about 15 people who were in here for 30 straight days, 18 hours a day, without getting sleep and stuff like that," he said.

The committee included police, fire, and ambulance officers, a public aid co-ordinator who advised on things like public health and evacuations, a public information officer, a provincial liaison, a parks and recreation construction representative, a public works officer, a water and waste co-ordinator, a city lawyer, the harbourmaster and a human resources officer to advise Reynolds on how much manpower he had at his disposal.

The city had been bracing itself since late in 1996, when the heaps of snow in Winnipeg and the deeper drifts in North Dakota guaranteed high water in the Red come spring thaw.

The Red had been high in the spring of 1996, too, and the city had used 300,000 sandbags that year. That wet spring left the ground saturated, so the city engineers knew they couldn't count on much of the meltwater being soaked up by the soil. By December 1996, there were meetings about the flood of 1997. "There was alarm already," Mayor Susan Thompson said. "There was going to be a hell of a lot of water."

The Sandbagger, an octopus-like machine, was working virtually around the clock.

A warning sign (opposite) was nearly submerged by April 25 as the rising Red made its way through Winnipeg.

CP photo

Wayne Glowacki

Jeff DeBooy

Jeff DeBooy

Homeowner John Kenny (above) gets a lift home from a naval reservist.

Navy Zodiacs (right) deliver sandbags.

In January 1997, Thompson ordered a million sandbags, more than three times what had been used in 1996. The city bought more bags in February and March, and had 1.4 million filled sandbags on hand by the time Grand Forks flooded. "In January, I remember some eyes being rolled at me when I asked for us to corner the market in the supply of sandbags," Thompson said later. "But the board of commissioners never argued with me." Filled to the two-thirds level with sand, each bag would weigh 45 pounds. Correctly stacked, with waterproof plastic sheeting incorporated, they would make effective emergency dikes for properties that weren't protected by the city's primary dike system. There are about 75 miles of primary dike in the city. Most primary dikes are roads, like Scotia Street and Kildonan and Bredin drives, but some are berms or parks. Primary dikes are built to 25.5 feet above winter river ice levels.

The city owned a Sandbagger, an octopus-like machine. Sand is poured into a rotating cone atop the octopus's "head" and is distributed through the machine's 12, not eight, arms. With a Sandbagger, a crew of 50 people can fill, tie and load 7,000 sandbags an hour. It was yet one more measure of the flood of 1997 that 7,000 sandbags an hour would be nowhere near enough. By the height of the crisis, seven of the machines would be working virtually around the clock in southern Manitoba.

The Sandbagger was the invention of Guy Bergeron, from St. Eustache, west of Winnipeg. He got the idea when he watched sandbags being filled along the Assiniboine in 1976, but it wasn't until 1991 that he developed a working model.

Winnipeg bought its Sandbagger in 1993 and Kamloops bought one in 1996. Grand Forks and East Grand Forks each bought one in early 1997 and Bergeron loaned his prototype to East Grand Forks. But when he offered four days' free use of yet another machine, Minneapolis, Fargo and Grand Forks all turned him down.

"They just say, 'No thanks. We don't think we need it,'" Bergeron said.

But not so in Winnipeg. In February, the city bought its second $26,000 Sandbagger.

And on April 20, the morning after she watched the TV pictures from Grand Forks, Thompson ordered another one million sandbags. The fear, even as early as January, was that the city would have plenty of sand but not enough bags. The lesson, said Thompson: "Always be over-prepared."

In the end, the city filled 6.5 million sandbags. Luckily, Winnipeg owns a sand pit near Birds Hill, a community near the Red River north of the city. Without the pit, Winnipeg would have been stuck

Staving off the Red on Lord Avenue.

paying $1.65 per sandbag, said Reynolds. At 6.5 million bags, the sand pit saved city taxpayers almost $11 million.

But even 6.5 million bags weren't enough. Reynolds built 14 earth dikes inside the city limits, in St. Norbert and along streets such as Lord Avenue, Hallama Drive and Rue des Trappistes. Those dikes were the equivalent of another one to 1.5 million sandbags.

On Friday, April 18, when Grand Forks still thought it would pull through, Reynolds was reading Alf Warkentin's latest predictions.

Warkentin hadn't so much changed the numbers as the emphasis. He said the high end of the forecasts was now the most likely outcome.

It was bad news for Reynolds, because the blizzard of April 5 and 6 had played havoc with sandbag-filling. "We were so far behind on making sandbags that we thought we'd never get it done," he said.

When the dikes failed in Grand Forks, Reynolds was watching TV at the city's flood headquarters. "That was scary as hell. The adrenalin was flowing. It hit us – this is real; this is coming at us."

95

This topographical map, modelled on one created by the city, identifies area vulnerable to flooding should water flow through or over dikes.

Leila Ave.

McPhillips St.

Red River

Perimeter Hwy.

Salter St.

Main St.

Inkster Blvd.

Henderson Hwy.

Lagimodiere Blvd.

King Edward St.

Notre Dame Ave.

St. James St.

Nairn Ave.

Regent Ave.

Archibald St.

Dugald Rd.

Marion St.

Portage Ave.

Assiniboine   River

Roblin Blvd.

Corydon Ave.

Osborne St.

Grant Ave.

Trans-Canada   Hwy.

Kenaston Blvd.

Bishop Grandin Blvd.

Wilkes Ave.

Lagimodiere Blvd.

Pembina Hwy.

St. Mary's Rd.

St. Anne's Rd.

McGillivray Blvd.

Waverley St.

Perimeter Hwy.

Perimeter Hwy.

N

Elevation above sea level

-740 ft.

740-750 ft.

750-760 ft.

760-770 ft.

770-780 ft.

780-790 ft.

790-800 ft.

Scale:

0   1   2   3   4   5 kms

PRIMARY DIKE

PERIMETER DIKE

ST. NORBERT EARTH DIKE

The city had less than two weeks to prepare or it could suffer the same fate, Reynolds said. He had already called twice-daily – morning and afternoon – meetings of his 15-member Emergency Preparedness and Co-ordination Committee. "I found it disturbing to hear people say that we wouldn't have a problem because our dikes are better," he said.

Reynolds had been commander of the military air base CFB Westwin until 1990, when rather than be transferred out of a city he and his wife had come to love, he hired on with the city as commissioner of parks, protection and culture.

Reynolds' military background was a boon when it came to coordinating operations between the military and the city authorities. Though his first encounter with Bob Meating wasn't a success – Meating had misread Reynolds and thought him poorly informed – the city's flood chief got on well with the military force in Winnipeg and got maximum co-operation from the soldiers.

"Once in uniform, you're never out of it," said Reynolds. "The military gives you a semblance of organization and process.

"When the military came in, they became part of our staff. They were great. Brig.-Gen. Rick Hillier was a real class act. I would say the military saved 120 to 150 houses, and that's a conservative guess."

It was one of many miracles in the spring of 1997 that Reynolds and Thompson worked through the flood crisis with no hint of a personality clash. Their history did not suggest so smooth a relationship. In May 1996, when Winnipeg was looking for a new police chief, Susan Thompson got the impression that Reynolds was gunning for the job. She promptly dropped him from the search committee – a move that Reynolds, who said he had never coveted the chief's job, took as an insult. Subsequently, Thompson tried but failed to get enough council support to fire a number of top bureaucrats, including Reynolds.

A member of the emergency committee, speaking anonymously in the aftermath, said it was to Reynolds' credit that the city's personnel all pulled in the same direction. "He doesn't sweat the small things. There was incredible pressure on him, but it didn't show," said the committee member. Instead of causing friction, the flood seemed to galvanize relationships, even among former adversaries. "If anything, people who didn't get along so well, got along better," said the committee member. Reynolds "has a fairly relaxed style. It's not all starched shirt. But he's not flippant either."

Said Reynolds: "There was rarely a time where we exercised any kind of authoritative discipline. We didn't have to. It doesn't work anyway, and it's not the way I operate."

Looking back at the flood, Thompson said it had been the first

opportunity in her five years in office for her and her staff to work towards a common goal. Up to then, she said, her policy of controlling costs and freezing property taxes had spawned resistance and resentment. The flood allowed no time for naysaying, said Thompson. "We simply had to move as a team, and we did. It was a case of everyone knowing what their role was and understanding what they were supposed to do. And not only that, they were darn good at it. Everybody rose to the occasion. The team held."

The city nipped one potentially fatal problem in the bud: There was no contour map of the city. Without knowing where the low spots were, city hall didn't know precisely where water would flow if it got through or over the dikes. But on April 19, while Grand Forks was going under, works commissioner Bill Carroll set the city's senior engineers to doing a topographical analysis. Later, when every sandbag counted, the information was invaluable. It told the city who should get sandbags first, and how many.

The city didn't need a map to know which areas were in the most immediate danger. Worst off were the people in St. Norbert, south of the floodway and permanent dike system. Not far behind were people on "the peninsula," a tight bend of the Red in St. Vital. Their addresses were on Kingston Row and Kingston Crescent.

Warkentin updated his forecast on Sunday, April 20, moving his prediction up to the high end of the range he had forecast 10 days earlier. "The south end of the city will have a problem," he said. "They might well be in trouble." It was the first warning that there would be flooding in Winnipeg. But that was nothing compared to the bombshell that followed – Ron Richardson's 11th-hour discovery of the Brunkild gap.

"This is unreal," Susan Thompson thought. "What's going on here?"

Thompson was already questioning every piece of information and advice she got, she said later. After all, Pat Owens, her counterpart in Grand Forks, had been assured her dikes were high enough. It wasn't until May 8, when the crest had passed and the city had taken everything nature could throw at it, that "my shoulders came down below my ear lobes," Thompson said.

"The south end of the city will have a problem," he said. "They might well be in trouble."

ALF WARKENTIN

The safety of the city depended on the massive Brunkild dike.

97

*Sandbagging
in St. Norbert.*

The city decided to build some insurance. If the floodwater found its way into the La Salle River basin, it would not crawl inexorably down on Winnipeg the way the Red River did. Instead, the La Salle would come roaring down on south Winnipeg. That's because the drop in elevation in the few miles from Brunkild to the floodway gate is 25 feet, almost exactly the same drop as from distant Emerson. The Red was a creeping giant; the La Salle would be a slashing torrent. The most immediate danger would be to 1,000 houses west of the Red and north of the floodway intake.

"We took four kilometres of dirt out of the Brady landfill," said Reynolds, "to make a dike from the Perimeter down Waverley, across the field to Rue des Trappistes, then to the primary dike on Pembina Highway." The four-foot-high dike was dubbed the L-dike because of its shape.

The city's criterion for ordering residents out of their homes was that water be within a foot of the main-floor elevation. Nobody in the city was in that position yet, but many were close and the river was still rising. On April 23, after Thompson's helicopter ride with Meating, the city warned 500 homeowners to be ready for an order to clear out within 24 hours. The next day, that number increased to 755.

As tensions grew, black humour began to surface on the city's emergency operation blackboard. Low Taxes, Low Dikes, read one. The Crest Hasn't Cleared Customs Yet, said another.

Thompson's skepticism about her information, it turned out, was misplaced. The combination of Warkentin's forecasts, the survey Bill Carroll had ordered and the work of Reynolds' emergency committee yielded predictions that were a quantum leap ahead of the bad advice Grand Forks Mayor Pat Owens had received.

As the crest entered Manitoba at Emerson on the last weekend in April and made its way to Winnipeg, it emerged that Warkentin had succeeded where entire teams of forecasters in the United States had failed.

The crest at Emerson arrived April 26 at 792.5 feet above sea level. Warkentin's forecast had called for 792 to 793.5 feet, and that was done after the blizzard but a week before Grand Forks was flooded.

The same April 10 forecast was also dead on for Morris. Warkentin was half a foot low for Ste. Agathe, but his revised forecasts of April 18 and 20 – after Grand Forks fell – made the correction.

His April 10 forecast was also accurate for Winnipeg, at the James Avenue pumping station, although he gave a very wide range at the time of 19.7 to 24.3 feet above the normal winter river ice level. By April 20, he had revised that to an estimated crest of 23.5 to 24.5 feet. The Red crested at 24.5 feet.

At 7 a.m. on Wednesday, April 23, while surveyors scrambled to find the optimum route for the Brunkild dike, Meating took Thompson by helicopter over the city and the Brunkild area.

He told her the situation was serious, but the priority was still southern Manitoba. Troops would move to Winnipeg as needed. But the fact was, nobody had ever seen a flood like this before.

"Even though I was confident in what the city was doing, I didn't want us to get caught. I went to see what it was about. Up in the air with the general instilled in me that he had a very good assessment of what was going on.

"The general gave me confidence that resources would come our way, but that the priority was southern Manitoba and when water reached Winnipeg, resources would be available. He knew the game plan."

Thompson could not be sure that Don Kuryk and his collection of private contractors and military engineers would win the race with the Red. In fact, that Wednesday morning, there were grave doubts within the Highways Department that the job could be done.

Energetic volunteers at work on Scotia Street on April 17.

Checking the dike (left) for leaks on Turnbull Drive.

Soldiers (opposite) were among the many volunteers shoring up protection for homes on Glenwood Crescent.

Wayne Glowacki

Jeff DeBooy

Warkentin puts a range on the crest forecasts, whereas the U.S. National Weather Service stubbornly tries to pinpoint the crest to a single figure. That's not a help to people planning defences against flooding.

Warkentin gave a range of dates when crests were to arrive; his American counterparts tried to pin it to a single day. Warkentin's approach was more useful because crests on flood plains tend to be gradual, more like hills than mountain peaks, climbing just a few inches the final days in a virtual plateau. It was important for residents to know that because it meant their dikes should be completed several days before an expected crest.

Warkentin had one more advantage: After the 1979 flood, he recalibrated his formula for calculating the effect of overland flooding. "It's very true that experience is the best teacher," he said.

The 24.5-foot level at James Avenue was an artificial crest – without Duff's Ditch, it would have gone much higher. The floodway gates were manipulated so the Red carried the maximum amount of water through Winnipeg that the city's dikes could be expected to hold back. That meant almost a week where the Red was at its record high level in Winnipeg and almost two weeks where it was above the level it had reached in any previous year – even the pre-floodway 1950.

That meant enormous strain on the emergency dikes, and it became a 24-hour-a-day job to plug leaks.

About 3,000 civic workers were redeployed from their normal duties to help fight the flood. For example, hundreds of people were plucked from their offices to staff the call centre that used up to 60 lines to answer the public's flood inquiries.

Everyone from city lawyers to engineers helped with the dike patrol

...it became a 24-hour-a-day job to plug leaks

Overcome by floodwaters at 410 Turnbull Dr.

Ken Gigliotti

– walking dikes searching for boils or leaks. The city's policy was that dikes be checked every 20 minutes.

Still, it came down to the volunteers.

"The city has 1,700 fewer employees than two years ago. If it wasn't for the volunteers, we wouldn't have been able to prepare. It's as simple as that. It was the volunteers that got us there," Reynolds said.

At one time there were 245 leaks in dikes protecting Winnipeg homes. Most of the leaks were not considered serious enough to be patched by building a new dike around them, so homeowners and the military kept the pumps going.

"You're going to have leaks in these sandbags. We had 375 pumps deployed that the city got, many of them lent to us. The coast guard (under Transport Canada) flew in two aircraft loads of pumps," Reynolds said.

"And of course, you had to get gas out there because in many cases the electricity had been turned off. So that became a huge logistics issue, particularly in the south end. We had a flotilla of 30 boats down there."

The city had about 150 pumps of its own, from sources such as the fire and sewer and waste departments. The rest were donated from other levels of government and from outside the province.

"Pumps became the big issue," Reynolds said. "I remember at one press conference, and someone's question was what do you need, and I held up a sign that said, 'Send Pumps.' "

Even earth dikes were under unbearable strain, both from the pressure of water pushing against them and from erosion by the currents. A clay dike protecting Turnbull Drive failed and so did some clay diking protecting Hallama Drive, which runs along the Seine River in southeast Winnipeg.

"You have to understand this isn't still water," Reynolds said. "It's not a lake. At one time south of the floodway we were recording the speed of the water from 25 to 30 kilometres per hour. Can you imagine?"

In total, 30 homes were lost to water.

"That's a small number when you look at the magnitude of the battle," Reynolds said.

The long-lasting artificial crest in Winnipeg meant weeks with the city's 70 sewer outfalls closed to keep the river from backing up into the sewer system. In case of a heavy rain, Winnipeg would have to rely on its 35 pumping stations to lift water directly into the river. But the pumps can handle only 35 to 50 per cent as much water as can flow out by gravity when the river is at normal levels. "We can handle a one-inch rainfall over five or six hours. That's a fairly intense storm," a waterworks engineer explained. But a bigger storm could overwhelm

"It's as simple as that. It was the volunteers that got us there."

LOREN REYNOLDS

While dikes (right) like this were needed on Scotia Street, the intense weight of the sandbags was a concern.

Joe Bryksa

the pumps.

In older parts of the city, where there is a combined sanitary and storm sewage system, the result would be raw sewage backing up into basements. In newer parts of the city, where there are separate systems for rainwater runoff and household wastes, the danger was less acute. But even there, a long cloudburst could overwhelm the storm sewers and get into the sanitary system through an unguarded manhole. Again, raw sewage in basements would be the result.

All over the city, homeowners cleared out their basements. And they searched for backflow valves and sewer plugs. A backflow valve is a floating ball enclosed so that it allows water to go down, but not up. A sewer plug is a disc, expandable by turning a wing-nut, that closes off the pipe under a toilet.

At Winnipeg Supply, one of the city's bigger hardware stores, the last week of April was madness. Clerks worked the phones like telemarketers, scouring the continent for valves that sold out as fast as they

Wayne Glowacki

Ralph Taupe worked hard to keep his Fort Garry home safe.

Jeff Debooy

Ken Reddig checks the water from the dike around his Glenwood Crescent home.

could stock the shelves. Eight clerks worked full-time just handling calls from worried homeowners, said Morris Matviychuk, the general manager.

Compression plugs that normally cost $8 were going for $38, if they could be found at all. "It's like roses on Valentine's Day," a plumber explained.

Winnipeg escaped the long, torrential downpour that would have caused city-wide basement flooding. But there was more than an inch of rain on May 7, and 47 homes in Fort Garry and River Heights had

sewage backup.

"It's not Chanel No. 5," said Emil Toma, who lives on Clarence Avenue in Fort Garry. The high-pressure sewage flow blew the ring off his basement catch basin, then began forcing its way through a shower and toilet, sending up a three-foot geyser that flooded his basement with a mixture of raw sewage and dying minnows.

Prodded by the impatient Brig.-Gen. Meating, the city, province and armed forces worked in late April on a plan to deal with the worst case – the collapse of the Brunkild dike, which would send up to

It was a team effort on Glenwood Crescent.

Packing up to leave home in St. Norbert (above).

60,000 cubic feet per second of water racing down on St. Norbert. In the worst of outcomes, it would wash away the four-foot-high L-dike that was St. Norbert's back-door protection, and knock out the primary and secondary dike systems. The water racing through the ruins of the Brunkild dike would make the La Salle River as big as the Red, and the Red was already higher than it had been since records began.

The emergency evacuation plan envisaged 150,000 Winnipeggers forced out of their homes. Three hospitals – St. Boniface General, Victoria General and the Riverview chronic-care complex – would have to be emptied.

But the city trusted that none of that would happen. It was a case of planning for the worst while hoping for the best. The detailed contingency plan was to have "in our hip pocket," in the words of the city's chief commissioner, Rick Frost.

Then came the weather forecast of Saturday, April 26. It called for high, sustained wind. Wind blowing steadily in the same direction across a lake like the one formed south of Winnipeg could churn up waves four feet high. Waves like that will chew through highways, railbeds and dikes as if they were made of sugar.

The wind began on Sunday, blowing up to nearly 40 miles an hour. On Monday, April 28, the city ordered the evacuation of St. Norbert – 2,352 homes – and the Kingston Row peninsula – 187 homes. St. Boniface General Hospital moved half its 500 patients to less-threatened city hospitals.

From the start of the flood crisis, Manitobans had looked for information and reassurance to Larry Whitney, an engineer in the Highways Department who had been pressed into service as EMO's chief spokesman. A week before, being pressed by reporters about the safety of Winnipeg, Whitney had searched for words to express his confidence in the floodway and the dikes. At last he found them.

"There will be no Grand Forks here," he said.

Now, Winnipeggers hoped Whitney was a prophet. Because, on the last day of April, with an eye on the storm-battered Brunkild dike, the city sent out more notices to prepare to evacuate. The notices went to every home along all three of the city's rivers – the Assiniboine, the Seine and the Red. With 2,500 homes already empty, the city was moving toward the greatest mass evacuation in its history – bigger than in the disastrous spring of 1950.

The April 30 warning notices went to 10,000 homes.

"There will be no Grand Forks here."

LARRY
WHITNEY

107

Residents of Grande Pointe had to use a boat to bring sandbags to their homes.

By April 25 (opposite) the Red was creeping up on the bridges near the forks of the Red and Assiniboine rivers.

Wayne Glowacki

CP photo

109

Wendy Carriere secures her home near the city.

CP photo

CP photo

CP photo

CP photo

Volunteer Ron Malkowich (far left) takes a well-earned break on a massive sandbag dike.

Downtown (above) as seen from St. Boniface.

City workers (left) seal an overflowing storm drain.

Diking the Bell family home (right), the closest to the floodway gates.

Ken Gigliotti

David Little (right) offers his labour on Scotia Street.

Young volunteers (far right) help build a 15-foot dike on Lord Avenue.

Joe Bryksa

Ken Gigliotti

CP photo

*Victoria Misiak
lays on lunch for
volunteers outside
her aunt's home
on Kingston Row.*

*The Red rises on the
Redwood Bridge.*

Jon Thordarson

*Checking the dikes on
Kingston Row.*

Ken Gigliotti

*All hands on deck
on Kingston Row
(above and right).*

Melanie Richard put her muscle to work on Scotia Street.

Diking homes on Scotia Street became a full-time job for many volunteers.

117

Soldiers kept dike-builders in sandbags on St. Mary's Road.

118

*Residents vigilantly scour
Scotia Street dikes
for breaches (left).*

*Baggers turned out by
the thousands across
the city (above).*

The floodway gates (above) on April 24.

Duff's Ditch
three days later (right).

Ken Gigliotti

Ken Gigliotti

Chapter Eight
THE STORM

IN EVERY diked community from Emerson to Winnipeg, floodfighters feared the three-day storm that gathered in late April. The wind would churn up whitecaps that would make boat travel – even with the big landing craft the navy was using in the valley – hazardous to impossible. The floodfighting crews in each town were pared down to the bare minimum needed to shore up the dikes. Everyone else – support staff, police, journalists – had to leave. If a ring dike failed, everybody in town would likely have to be lifted out by helicopter.

By late Sunday, April 27, the wind was whipping across the flood lake at up to 40 miles an hour. In Ottawa, Prime Minister Jean Chretien had called a general election. Most of Manitoba, too busy to be angry or to get involved, ignored the call.

In St. Jean, Flo Beaudette looked to the town's defences. The dike that ringed St. Jean was at 788 feet; the water was at 783.96. Beaudette hoped four feet would be enough freeboard. He knew four-foot waves were a possibility. And he worried about his now-vacated farm. Already, a quarter of the diked farms in the valley had gone under and Beaudette knew there would be more before the storm ended.

The wind blew all day Monday.

And early Tuesday, it scored its first major victory, breaking through the dike west of Ste. Agathe. Ste. Agathe does not count as one of the valley's ring-diked communities; it's considered too high to need one. But it had a temporary ring dike and, like the other towns in the valley, it had been cleared of all but the essential floodfighters, 22 of them.

"You could hear the water coming, flowing over like rapids," said postmaster Jean Champagne, who was the last man out of Ste. Agathe that stormy morning.

"And it was night, so it was amplified and more scary. When the

Photo courtesy of Emergency Management Organization.

water started coming, it was the beginning of the end."

Said RCMP Const. Richard Brault, who boated into Ste. Agathe after daylight to bring out the 22 floodfighters: "Within an hour, the whole town was submerged in water. There was three to six feet there," he said. "The waves were two to two and half feet high. There were whitecaps."

"It was unexpected, really," Champagne said. "We thought we had control on the east (river) side and it came from the west. It was a little surprise attack from the rear."

Overland flooding from the direction of Rosenort jumped Highway 75, washed out a section of railroad near the centre of Ste. Agathe that was acting as a natural dike and barrelled into the town, 25 miles south of Winnipeg.

The morning the dikes failed in Ste. Agathe.

As the winds picked up, (opposite) soldiers skidded their way across the dike at Ste. Agathe.

"You could hear the water coming, flowing over like rapids."
POSTMASTER
JEAN CHAMPAGNE

Joe Bryksa

Joe Bryksa

Joe Bryksa

Ste. Agathe
residents (above)
thought they had
taken every
precaution.

Unfortunately,
nothing escaped
destruction
(far right).

Waves (opposite)
relentlessly pounded
the Ste. Agathe
dike on May 8.

The railway and highway were the last holes in the temporary ring
dike to be closed and were lower than the rest of the dike. The skele-
ton crew of floodfighters were shoring up the breach along the highway about 11:30 p.m. Monday when they noticed water pouring in
through the tracks. "We were working there and someone in the
group said, 'We have this water building up' and then we heard the
words, 'It's coming. Let's hightail it out of here,'" Champagne said.
When the onrushing water blew out the plug on the railway tracks,
said Champagne, it sounded "like a bladder bursting." Within hours,
the homes of 500 people were destroyed.

At 3 a.m., a telephone call woke Harold Clayton, the EMO director.
It was to tell him that Ste. Agathe had been lost. It was a bitter
moment for Clayton. "We thought the community had taken every
precaution," he said.

At 6:30 a.m., Clayton phoned Reeve Bob Stefaniuk of the RM of
Ritchot, the municipality that takes in Ste. Agathe. An evacuee,
Stefaniuk was staying at the Crowne Plaza hotel in Winnipeg. He was
already awake when Clayton's call came through.

"I was shocked," he said. "I couldn't believe it. It was a very bad day."
Stefaniuk hurried over to the EMO war room on the top floor of
the Woodsworth Building to learn what details he could of the disaster. "The weather was dreary, cold that morning," Stefaniuk said.

Joe Bryksa

Charles Wiens tosses sandbag to Trish Baudry at her home along Hwy. 305 near Ste. Agathe.

Once the dike gave way the village was swamped within an hour (below and far right).

Ken Gigliotti

Joe Bryksa

Joe Bryksa

"Psychologically, it was very bad for everyone."

With the pessimism born of exhaustion, Clayton felt the same way. He resigned himself to more such calls as the storm wore on. If Ste. Agathe had flooded, why not others?

Instead, the ring dikes around the towns held. But hundreds of buildings – mostly farm homes but also including an elementary school, a seniors' home and Evangelical Mennonite Church near Rob Eidse's home in Riverside – fell to the wind-whipped flood. Eidse fought round the clock and stayed dry. But 14 neighbouring farm homes fell victim to the water.

Eidse complained bitterly about how the military wanted him to evacuate, threatening to arrest him if he didn't. "If all the people who told me I had to leave just helped me with my dike," he said, "I'd be a lot better off and they wouldn't have to worry about me."

At least a dozen homes were lost on the southern fringe of Letellier, as water from the Pembina River joined forces with the swollen Marais River.

Outside Rosenort, a ring-diked town on the Morris River, Myron Dueck and his father Irvin battled the bone-chilling wind to shore up the sandbag dike that ringed their farm home. Their materials were sandbags that they collected by boat from neighbours' farms where the dikes had fallen. At least 60 farms in the RM of Morris, which includes Rosenort, were flooded during the storm.

"It's like that movie, Alive," Myron said. "You eat the dead. It's just fight, that's all it is. It's very hard to take."

A few hours later, in St. Jean, a volunteer firefighter, looking through binoculars, saw the north side of the town's ring dike being chipped away. A backhoe got to the spot in time and shored it up. Flo Beaudette figures it was this day, April 29, that his farm lost its first battle with the Red in 120 years. The water breached his ring dike, buckled the farmhouse floor and destroyed his new $20,000 kitchen. He can't be sure of the date, because no one was there. His brothers had been ordered out by the EMO and the farm had to be left on its own. Flo was certain that if somebody could have stayed behind to watch the dike and keep the pump going, the farm would have survived. He was bitter then and he was still bitter long after the water had gone down.

But it was at the south end of Winnipeg that the stakes were highest. At 6 a.m. on April 29, two hours before military, city and provincial planners were scheduled to start work on their contingency for a breach of the Brunkild dike, the phone rang at Ron Richardson's home at Oak Bluff.

His wife, Barb, called him out of the shower. It looked like the plan-

"If all the people who told me I had to leave just helped me with my dike, I'd be a lot better off and they wouldn't have to worry about me."
ROB EIDSE

Richard Dorge could only grab a few necessities when he was rescued from the rising water at his farm near Ste. Agathe.

127

ning session might be too late. It looked like the worst might already be happening.

The caller was Guy Cooper, the Highway Department's head of dike construction. The water had climbed five feet over night and was only six inches from the top of the dike. With the wind still howling and waves pounding on the dike, it looked like a major breach was imminent.

Earlier in the storm, the wind had been blowing from the west, possibly contributing to the loss of Ste. Agathe. But at some time between the bursting of the dike at Ste. Agathe and the alarming phone call to Richardson, the wind had shifted and was coming from the south.

It had blown that way long enough to "set up" the lake. That meant the surface of the water was no longer horizontal – the wind had tilted it so that it was 15 inches higher at the north end. The 15-inch set-up was part of the sudden rise, five to six feet, that Cooper told Richardson about.

"We almost lost it here," said Richardson, drawing an X on a map showing the spot on the original dike, 7.5 miles south of La Salle.

"We had backhoes working constantly in here. It wasn't an area of high fill originally. Just dig out one side of the road, pile it on the other, and run back and forth over it with a bulldozer to compact it. That was the closest call we ever had there."

It was touch and go all that day. At noon, Andy Horosko, the deputy minister who had come up with the idea of the schoolbus breakwater, arrived at the legislature to brief the Filmon cabinet. He was, said a water resources official who saw him heading in to the meeting, "as white as a sheet."

The crew on the Brunkild dike figured they could handle a breach of 30,000 cubic feet per second – roughly half the flow of the Red River at its highest and roughly half the flow that would result if the dike failed completely. But they would have to handle it quickly. From Brunkild to the floodway gates, the drop is 25 feet – almost exactly what the Red drops in its long, meandering crawl from Emerson. A breach of the Z-dike would send high water down the La Salle to St. Norbert in five hours. With waves threatening them every step of the way, Kuryk and his crew kept working, making the Brunkild Z-dike higher and stronger.

Surveyor Bob McIntyre kept a close eye on the Z-dike near Domain.

Looking southward from the floodway gates on April 30.

Ken Gigliotti

Gary Filmon toured the valley as the winds picked up and knew the worst of the flood was reaching its zenith.

"This was a period of five days of white-knuckle time," he said. "The reason was, with that switch of the wind to the south that day, it took our helicopter an hour to fly from Winnipeg to Emerson. We were bucking that incredible head wind. When we got to Emerson, there were two things that were apparent. One was, we were already seeing erosion on the south side of the dike and that was just six hours in to that wind. Secondly, there was a differential water level of a foot from the south side of Emerson to the north side of Emerson.

"We were really worried because Brunkild dike had a lot of water on it and it wasn't completed yet. They hadn't had time to bring in plastic or snow fencing or boom or anything to protect it. A lot of us felt nervous that day."

Though the waves made it impossible to tell for sure, it appeared the Red peaked in Emerson during the storm on Sunday. And on Tuesday, April 29, the water went down. The river dropped only an inch and a half, but it lifted spirits from the border to Winnipeg. "I think the North (from Emerson to Winnipeg) was waiting to see what would come through the border," said Emerson's mayor, Wayne Arseny. "I think it would have been tremendously demoralizing for the rest of Manitoba if we hadn't held." Emerson's dikes also protected the border hamlet of Noyes, Minn., – 10 houses and customs offices – but the

Plastic sheets were used (left) to protect earthen dikes.
Premier Gary Filmon (above) toured the valley as the winds gathered force.

basements in Noyes all flooded because there was no electricity to run sump pumps.

Just as cheering as the drop, however minuscule, in the river level was the news that the crest had been 18 inches lower than predicted.

The sun shone Thursday morning on the beginning of a new month – it was May 1 – and on the most hopeful day the province had seen since the blizzard nearly a month before. The Red was within inches of its crest in Winnipeg, and it probed – as it was to keep probing for nearly two more weeks – for soft spots in the city's flood defences.

Three apartment blocks – two on Pembina Highway and one on Roslyn Road – had to be evacuated after dikes failed, as did six single-family houses. The 113-unit block at 21 Roslyn was evacuated after the Assiniboine River found its way into the basement, threatening to reach the building's electrical panel. About 100 people had to leave their homes in The Ports, 1660 Pembina Highway, when the Red burst the building's dike.

Resident Ronald Warner said he and his neighbours had been warned the sandbag dike might burst, and they had all made arrangements for shelter.

When the dike caved in at about 3:30 p.m. May 1, 11 pumps were working in the basement to get rid of seepage. It was one of 92 calls to trouble spots on the city dikes that day. Of those, nine were serious.

But good news was on the way. There had been a fierce debate within the Water Resources Branch about how serious a breach of the Brunkild dike would be. Opting to err on the side of caution, the city had sent out warning notices to 10,000 households. But on May 1, the engineers took another look at the numbers. Their verdict was that the city could handle a 30,000-cubic-feet-per-second breach in the dike – enough water could be diverted into the floodway to make room in the Red's channel for the water coming into the city from the west. There was also the comforting news that the Red was topping out a foot and a half lower than everyone had feared.

The city cancelled the evacuation alert.

"He and his neighbours had been warned the sandbag dike might burst."

RONALD WARNER

City cyclists (left) are forced to carry their bikes.

The Assiniboine River (far left) backs up into a Wellington Crescent apartment building.

131

Chapter Nine
THE ELECTION

THERE WAS no pressing need for a federal election in the spring of 1997. The Liberal administration of Jean Chretien had 18 months to go in the mandate it won in 1993. Parliament was not deadlocked. There was no constitutional crisis. But in Ottawa, an election was in the air.

"I am 99.999999 per cent sure that it's going to be an early June election," John Harvard, the Liberal member of Parliament for Winnipeg-St. James told *Free Press* national reporter Dan Lett on April 10. "The only thing left undone at this point is the announcement."

Opinion polls showed Chretien's Liberals with a comfortable popularity margin. But the prime minister couldn't admit he was calling a snap vote out of sheer opportunism. The party line, which Harvard trotted out in his conversation with Lett, was that the other parties had already begun the campaign so it would be best to call the vote and get it over with. Otherwise, the country would endure what amounted to a six-month election campaign.

There was little enthusiasm for the election in Manitoba. The province was still digging itself out from the April 5 and 6 blizzard and it was already a given that there would be overland flooding in the Red River Valley. Then came the Grand Forks debacle of April 19, the event that told most of Manitoba the 1997 flood would be a serious threat to life and property. Even the Manitoba Liberal caucus began to get cold feet.

In Ottawa, Lett began what would become weeks of persistent calls to Elections Canada, the office that oversees the carrying out of federal elections. Among its chores are creating the voters' list, hiring returning officers and enforcing the rules on campaign spending. There is a section in the Elections Act that provides for the chief electoral officer to make a recommendation to cabinet that voting be delayed in a constituency if conditions are such that balloting can't be full and fair. Lett

wanted to know if the head of Elections Canada, Jean-Pierre Kingsley, would consider that option in Manitoba. It looked like the flood would be a major upset for the constituencies of Provencher and Portage-Lisgar – the Red River is the boundary between them. It also looked like the effects would be severe in Winnipeg South, which takes in St. Norbert.

Was Kingsley aware of the discretionary powers the Elections Act gave him? Was he aware of the wall of water surging down through North Dakota to the Canadian border? There was no way of knowing.

All indications were that Chretien would call the election April 27 – the first time a Canadian election campaign would begin on a Sunday – and the country, with or without parts of Manitoba, would go to the polls June 2.

On Thursday, April 24, coming up on the weekend when Chretien was expected to call the election, MPs David Iftody and Reg Alcock led a Liberal caucus appeal to put off the vote until the flood situation stabilized. Iftody, whose Provencher riding figured to be – and was – the hardest hit, said, "I think a delay is a good idea." Said Alcock, the MP for Winnipeg South: "I would rather be helping people sandbagging than campaigning." Ron Duhamel, from St. Boniface, and David Walker, from Winnipeg North Centre, supported Iftody and Alcock in their appeal to the Liberal caucus. New Democrat Bill Blaikie, from Transcona, also asked Chretien to delay the election.

Prime Minister Jean Chretien's visit (opposite) to Manitoba on April 26 – exemplified by this crushing scrum on Scotia Street – was hastily conceived and poorly executed.

"I would rather be helping people sandbagging than campaigning."

REG ALCOCK

The answer was no. The Liberals would go to the polls at the absolute earliest opportunity. Kingsley's office was working on a permanent voters' list, a first for Canada. The list would be official on Saturday, April 26, so Chretien would call the election the next day.

The Elections Act called for a 36-day campaign, shorter than ever before. So the election would be called April 27 and held June 2, come hell or high water.

Liberals held 12 of Manitoba's 14 seats in the Parliament that Chretien was planning to dissolve. Traditional voting patterns had gone out the window in the ABC – Anybody But the Conservatives – election of 1993. The Conservatives were trampled down to two seats – one in Quebec and one in New Brunswick. The Liberals couldn't expect to hang on to 12 Manitoba seats, but with any luck, they thought they could hang on to eight or nine. They wouldn't help their luck by having it appear that Chretien either didn't know or didn't care that the flood of the century was coming down the Red River Valley. The prime minister would have to come to Manitoba.

Chretien meets the people at St. Adolphe.

Or maybe it wasn't a matter of paving the way for the election. Lloyd Axworthy, the senior Liberal in the Manitoba caucus, the minister of foreign affairs and the MP for Winnipeg South Centre, said it was not. Axworthy said he invited Chretien to Winnipeg to assess the flood, and to give Axworthy the authority to reduce red tape to get a new flood disaster agreement with the province, and to deal with other matters flood victims might have, such as filing income tax forms on time or getting employment insurance advances.

"Instead, it got turned into sort of a major public issue," Axworthy said. "He did not come to Manitoba to assess the question of the election. The planning of the election had already been taken. It was not a practical question to shut down a $20-million campaign which, in effect, had already started."

Whatever the motivation, Chretien's visit to Manitoba on Saturday, April 26, was hastily conceived and poorly executed.

Gary Filmon, not without some pleasure at watching the Liberals

squirm, called it "an advance person's nightmare. I'm convinced the prime minister made the decision to come here on very short notice, probably with great pressure from people within his campaign organization."

Filmon was at 17 Wing that Saturday morning to meet Chretien. He and Bob Meating had their verbal sparring match while they waited for the prime minister's Challenger to land. It was a cold morning and grey clouds hung low over the city and the great expanse of water to the south.

Chretien's plane was an hour and a half late. "He had been speaking the night before in New Brunswick," Filmon said later, "and they put him on the Challenger and instead of stopping in Ottawa, he came right through to Winnipeg. He was tired, no question. He was probably exhausted because of what he had been doing, obviously, in preparation for the election announcement the next day. And yet, as always, he was friendly."

The plan was for Chretien to fly out by helicopter for a look at the flooding in the south. But it was too dangerous because of the low ceiling – no military officer wanted to take responsibility for flying Chretien and getting him killed or maimed in a crash.

So he and Filmon had an unscheduled chat for about an hour on flood compensation. Meanwhile, Chretien's handlers arranged a convoy by road to St. Adolphe so the prime minister could at least see the edge of the flood. At St. Adolphe, where he arrived about 10:15 a.m., he met sandbaggers from a nearby Hutterite colony and from the Royal 22nd Regiment, the Van Doos. He met local officials but didn't hold anything that could be described as a discussion. "We thought we'd have a chance for a few words, but it didn't occur," said Bob Stefaniuk, reeve of the RM of Ritchot. But "you could see by the expression on his face he was taken back and realized how enormous the situation was."

The convoy rolled back to Winnipeg. As it crossed the St. Vital Bridge, Filmon was astounded that they didn't turn off to see Kingston Row, the most endangered part of the city except for the outlying areas outside the primary dikes.

On their way back into the city, heading into south St. Vital, Filmon thought it would be an appropriate time for Chretien to see the sandbagging efforts along Kingston Crescent and Kingston Row. Instead, the motorcade sped right past over the St. Vital Bridge.

"I thought, quite honestly, we were going to stop in and see Kingston Row," Filmon said. "And I didn't know why we were being taken right by and going right through to Scotia. Clearly, they had set up an event there." Indeed they had. The TV cameras and the

Troops showed the prime minister flood precautions taken at St. Adolphe.

Manitoba campaign leaders were waiting on Scotia Street, at the home of a party supporter where sandbagging was going on.

At Scotia Street and Jefferson Avenue, the scene was already confused. Print, radio and TV reporters from across the country were waiting, having gathered more than an hour earlier. A couple of satellite trucks had been set up to beam Chretien's tour live to TV sets around the country. In the back along the river, sandbagging efforts were in full swing, overseen by city engineers who were giving volunteers crash courses on how to lay bags.

When Chretien pulled up, it was virtual pandemonium as reporters, photographers, TV cameramen and sound people descended. In media parlance, it's called scrumming. But the scramble on Scotia Street was the mother of all scrums.

Chretien with Winnipeg Mayor Susan Thompson.

"It was so chaotic, as I got out of the car I got knocked over before I had gone 100 feet," Filmon said. "Someone grabbed me before I hit the ground. Another 100 feet further, I got smashed into a truck by a guy with a big video TV camera. At that point I decided I couldn't keep up with the mob, and that there was no point to my keeping up with the mob. No one was interested in talking to me anyway. So I just stayed on the street."

Chretien, ushered by his handlers and surrounded by beefy bodyguards, weaved through the marauding media to where the sandbaggers were working, making his way to the back deck of Katarina Sajatovic's house at 301 Scotia. There, she tied an orange ribbon around his left arm, the same ribbon sandbagging captains wore, to show his solidarity with Manitobans.

Standing next to Chretien was Kevin Lamoureux, Liberal member of the Manitoba legislature.

Then Chretien, wearing dress loafers, beige corduroy trousers and a dark brown leather jacket, was led down to the mucky, soaking-wet dike. Someone handed him a sandbag.

"What do you want me to do with this?" he asked.

"Throw it here," someone answered. So he did, into the arms of lawyer Richard Good, the co-chairman of the federal Liberal election campaign in Manitoba.

And then, after a few words with reporters, he was gone, to meet up with a military helicopter in Kildonan Park. The sky had cleared enough to fly out over southern Manitoba.

Pandemonium ruled as the prime minister toured Scotia Street.

"What do you want me to do with this?" He asked.

JEAN CHRETIEN

This infamous photo — typical of superficial politicking — exposed Chretien to critics nationwide who saw it reflecting a callous leader out of touch with the magnitude of the crisis in Manitoba.

CP photo

Foreign Affairs Minister Lloyd Axworthy was already home campaigning in Winnipeg.

"It didn't make much sense to campaign in a row boat," **Axworthy recalled 18 years later.**

"I don't know why anyone would attempt to handle it that way, but they did," Filmon said. "It was an unfortunate event. I think he didn't get good advice on that one."

The image, that of superficial photo-op politicking, was flashed across the nation's TV screens that night and discussed in opinion columns across the country the next day. It was not a great moment for the prime minister or his party. It probably damaged Chretien more than it did the party, which went on to form another majority government, albeit reduced in numbers, after the election. But the sandbag photo opportunity added to the image of Chretien as callous, shallow and out of touch. It may have played a part in the groundswell of opinion in June that, although Chretien had led the party to electoral victory, it was time for him to leave the political stage.

Back in Ottawa on Sunday, the day after the sandbag incident, Chretien went to Rideau Hall to ask for an election to be called. When he emerged, reporters asked him why he was going to the polls with so much time left in his mandate. He looked confused and had to refer to notes. His answer was a restatement of the argument Harvard had put forward two weeks earlier – that the other parties had already begun campaigning.

The challenge for Manitoba politicians was not to be seen as politicking, particularly in the flood zone. Alcock, the Liberal in Winnipeg South, had already warned his supporters he wouldn't campaign at the beginning. "I think that at a time when so many people are threatened, people's minds are, and should be, on making sure everybody is safe," he said.

Alcock was taking a leaf out of the book of another Liberal politician up for election during another flood. There was a federal election in 1979, another flood year, albeit not as bad as 1997. The Liberal candidate in Winnipeg-Fort Garry was a young former MLA looking for his first seat in Parliament. His name was Lloyd Axworthy. Axworthy recognized it would be better to be seen fighting the flood than fighting the Conservatives.

"It didn't make much sense to campaign in a rowboat," Axworthy recalled 18 years later. "There's a human factor which is such that if there is a threat of a community being flooded, you have to stop and help out." The 1979 election was a squeaker, but Axworthy edged Sidney Spivak, a former provincial Conservative leader.

In the years that followed, south Winnipeg became his fiefdom and Axworthy was the surest bet in the Liberal stable when the 1997 race was called.

His cabinet job – he was minister of foreign affairs – had him in China when the April 5 blizzard struck. He had planned to be back in

Winnipeg that weekend for a wedding, but when he got to Vancouver from Beijing, there were no flights to Winnipeg – the storm had closed Winnipeg International Airport. Axworthy flew to Washington instead. Among his appointments was one with Madeleine Albright, the U.S. secretary of state. He suggested, and she agreed, they should consult more about cross-border water matters – including the flood-prone Red River.

When he got back to Ottawa, Axworthy began some groundwork – meeting with the Defence Department to see what troops would be available to help out in Manitoba and speeding up some negotiations with the province to close the books on the 1993 flooding of the Assiniboine. There had been a long dispute over how the affected municipalities would be compensated.

Then came the disaster in Grand Forks, and the co-ordination work took on fresh urgency. The blizzard made it obvious there would be a call for federal aid; the bursting dikes in Grand Forks said the flooding would be serious and Manitoba would need every bit of help it could get. After Chretien's April 26 trip to Winnipeg, Axworthy sought carte blanche to cut bureaucratic corners. "I need a full mandate from you," he told Chretien. "It's not just enough for me to be able to pick up the phone and talk to some minister of another department. I need to do it with your authority." Chretien agreed.

Axworthy would need the prime minister's blessing; Gary Filmon had already served notice that there would be no holds barred in federal-provincial negotiations.

On April 23, three days before Chretien's visit and four days before the open-secret election call, Filmon denounced the federal aid formula in general and Axworthy's colleague Doug Young, the minister of defence, in particular. The premier's complaint was that the federal formula was generous once a disaster occurred, but it was stingy with measures that could prevent a disaster. The federal government would pick up 90 per cent of disaster costs over a $5-million threshold, but it would pay only about 16 per cent of a municipality's costs of shoring up a permanent ring dike, for example.

"Here we have an opportunity for people to make a small investment ahead of time in preparation and protection against the flood, and by building ring dikes to stop the floodwater we are potentially saving half a billion dollars," Filmon said. "But he (Young) won't even put forward five or six million to help the municipal governments to invest in the right things to protect themselves against the floodwaters."

Axworthy thought Filmon's frustrations would have been better aimed at the chartered banks. The municipalities were in a credit

Jeff DeBooy

crunch as they tried to raise their dikes and lay in supplies of sandbags. "I take it with a little salt," Axworthy said later, "when I see some banks out there being so patriotic supporting flood relief, but they were still calling in credit lines in those early days."

But though they sniped in public, Filmon and Axworthy negotiated in private and signed a memorandum of understanding on May 1, barely a week after Filmon had thrown down the gauntlet. It was to lead to more specific agreements that would get money flowing into flood victims' pockets. It was also destined to be the source of some of the bitterest federal-provincial fighting in years.

As Filmon and Axworthy drafted their memorandum, Jean-Pierre Kingsley, the chief federal elections officer, took up Filmon's invitation to come out to Manitoba to see the flooding first-hand. The question of whether to delay the election for some ridings was still hanging and there had been no indication from Kingsley what he would decide, or

Premier Gary Filmon tours the Brunkild dike.

Gen. Brock Horseman, deputy commander of Air Command, meets the prime minister, his wife Aline and Axworthy at CFB Winnipeg.

when he would decide it. Iftody's and Alcock's opponents said a campaign while the area was under water was unfair because it favoured the incumbents. The challengers wouldn't be able to get their names known because nobody dared approach voters. But the mood of the electors, so far as *Free Press* reporters could assess it, was that they wanted to vote with the rest of Canada. A delayed vote, they said, would skew the campaign. If Chretien won a majority, their votes would be rendered unimportant. If he were on the edge of a majority, or if one of the other parties were on the edge of gaining official status in the House of Commons, their vote would have inflated importance, and they didn't want that, either.

Kingsley arrived in Winnipeg late on May 2, a Friday, and toured the

140

flooded valley the next day with Filmon. He announced his decision at a press conference in Winnipeg on Sunday.

There would be no delay.

The *Free Press* had decided to take two opinion samples during the election campaign, so it was the work of a moment to piggyback a couple of flood-related questions onto the list that Probe Research was posing. Probe was in the field from May 2 to 7 asking, among other things, whether Kingsley had made the right move, whether the flood had affected voting intentions, and if so, how.

The results revealed an angry province.

Kingsley had been wrong, the respondents said – he should have delayed the entire election. And for a third of the respondents, Chretien's early call had changed their voting intentions. About 34 per cent of those said they would switch away from the Liberals; others said they would now boycott the election. That was the bad news for the Liberals, but it was tempered by the fact that the party had started so far out in front that they could absorb some backlash.

Chretien made one trip to Winnipeg during the campaign – his where-do-I-throw-the-sandbag visit doesn't count because the campaign didn't begin until the next day.

He came on Wednesday, May 20, and Filmon let it be known he expected the centrepiece of the visit would be Chretien's signature guaranteeing half the funding for a $270-million flood measures program.

The Liberals took no chances on another Scotia Street debacle. This time, the venue was the Billy Bishop Building at 17 Wing, the home of Air Command. A more secure venue would be hard to find. There would be no embarrassing protesters. And the setup – Chretien on a platform with Axworthy and Susan Thompson – meant there would be no reporters' scrum like the one on Scotia Street where Filmon, and Axworthy too, were nearly knocked down.

But Chretien wasn't in Winnipeg to commit to $135 million in spending. There was still no deal, the Liberals said. Yes there was, said the Filmon Tories, and showed a letter from Don Leitch, Manitoba's top civil servant, to Roger Bilodeau, a senior federal bureaucrat. Leitch's three-page letter went into detail on how the $270 million would be spent, and gave the impression that a deal had been made and was waiting only to be announced. The day before Chretien's trip, Liberal backbenchers like Alcock and Iftody had been expecting him to make an announcement.

In the aftermath of the trip, Axworthy said Leitch's letter was a "wish list" and the province was playing politics and creating unreasonable expectations by making it public.

Jean-Pierre Kingsley, chief federal elections officer, came out to see the flooding first-hand.

Kingsley had been wrong, the respondents said – he should have delayed the entire election.

CP photo

141

Alcock turned his constituency office into a flood relief centre.

Then defence minister Doug Young toured the flooded Red River Valley with local MP David Iftody.

Late in the campaign, the *Free Press* ran its second poll. This time, it threw out the question about Kingsley's decision but posed the same question about the early election call. Again, a third of respondents said the timing had influenced their voting decisions, but this time the anger seemed more sullen and directed less at Chretien and the Liberals than at politics and politicians in general.

When the votes were counted June 2, Iftody and Alcock kept their seats. Across the river, the Reform party's Jake Hoeppner kept his seat, too, turning back what had been expected to be an overwhelming challenge from Brian Pallister, the Conservative. The New Democratic Party knocked off Liberals in north Winnipeg and northern Manitoba, Reform took Dauphin-Swan River from the Liberals and the Conservatives took Brandon-Souris, also from the Liberals. But of those changes, only Hoeppner's victory in Portage-Lisgar figured as a surprise. In the end, it looked like Manitobans had set aside the emotions the flood had sparked and voted pretty much the way they would have in a dry spring.

Nationally, the flood highlighted the opportunism of the Liberal election call. At the beginning of the campaign, reporters across the country were asking about the emergency in Manitoba and its effect on the vote. By the end of the campaign, they were asking forceful questions about the timing of the election and the early call. Chretien and the Liberals looked bad as they struggled for a palatable answer. The flood also served to make the election the No. 2 story in the country. That meant less discussion of the issues, an advantage for the Liberals. The net result was that nationally as well as in Manitoba, the flood probably did not play a major role in the election.

But federal-provincial relations were a different story. In the storm over the meaning of Don Leitch's letter, each side had come close to calling the other a liar. It would take a long time to clear the poisoned air.

It would take a long time to clear the poisoned air.

Reform MP Jake Hoeppner pulled a surprise election victory in Portage-Lisgar.

Chapter Ten
RED RIVER RELIEF

I T WAS March and Winnipeg was still in the grip of winter, but David Luginbuhl was thinking about spring. Specifically, Lt.-Col. David Luginbuhl of the Salvation Army was thinking about the spring thaw and all the water that was going to come down the Red River.

On a Wednesday morning in late March, Luginbuhl, who is the Army's divisional commander for Manitoba and Northwestern Ontario, was on the phone to fellow Salvationists in Minneapolis and Chicago. He was looking for SACs – Salvation Army canteens. When it comes to feeding flood refugees or lines of hungry sandbaggers, there is no substitute for these mobile kitchens. Luginbuhl hoped to get his hands on three or four. At the height of the crisis, he commanded a fleet of 67 of them.

Luginbuhl had also notified the province in March that if Red River Valley residents had to be moved to Winnipeg, the Booth Centre would be able to feed 250 people every 35 minutes.

"We're planning for the worst and hoping for the best," Luginbuhl said. It was as well they did. Less than two weeks later, the heaviest blizzard in Manitoba's history ratcheted the flood crisis up several notches. And in less than a month, Grand Forks would be in ruins, the largest evacuation in Manitoba's history would be under way and the Salvation Army would be helping to battle the flood of the century.

Besides equipment, Luginbuhl wanted experience for his troops. On April 9, he led a team to North Dakota, where they helped Fargo turn back the flood. The Winnipeg Sally Ann crew met with Salvationists who had fought the good fight in Breckenridge, Minn. and Wahpeton, N.D., a few days before. From Fargo, the Winnipeggers went down the river to Grand Forks for an eight-day battle with the Red that ended in defeat and heartbreak.

Luginbuhl had already started stockpiling blankets, boots and the like. On April 15, the Canadian Imperial Bank of Commerce started taking cash donations for the Army's flood campaign, dubbed We Care.

The response, even for people whose business is miracles, was staggering.

The Red Cross, which became the main conduit for flood relief donations, took in $10 million in cash and merchandise from corporate donors. The Salvation Army brought in another $4 million from companies. Some corporations mounted three-pronged aid efforts – cutting cheques, organizing employee campaigns, then matching the staff donations.

Individual donors were just as generous; they gave $11 million.

Eight-year-old Carissa Ilyniak of Winnipeg sent $1.88. "Even though I am still a little girl I think I could help by donating a little bit of money to the (people) who need it," she wrote in a letter accompanying her donation.

"No onc is saying no," Anne Bennett, the We Care spokeswoman, said in late April. The Army issued a tax receipt for donations over $10, but Bennett said most of the corporate donors of goods and services didn't ask for a receipt or documentation. The list of donors ran to 10 pages. "Most of them will never receive public recognition," Bennett said. "They're doing it because they care about their community." In fact, the Salvation Army and the Red Cross were reluctant to name any donors because of the impossibility of naming them all. A $500 donation from a two-employee shop was just as praiseworthy as a $100,000 cheque from a bank, Bennett pointed out.

Some of the corporate stars were: McGavin Foods Ltd., which donated the bread for the 30,000 sandwiches a day the Salvation Army distributed to sandbaggers and refugees; Body Shop stores, which gave $100,000 worth of soaps; National Leasing, which loaned six trucks for transporting food to sandbagging sites; Sears Canada, which loaned a

The Salvation Army (opposite) brought together a stockpile of supplies and opened a flood relief centre.

Volunteer Jim Browning had his work cut out for him with a raft of donated goods from Oklahoma City.

fleet of company trucks, and organized, with CJOB Radio, the sale of $250,000 worth of Flood Relief T-shirts; Greyhound Airlines, which flew volunteers into Manitoba free of charge; Pepsi and Coca-Cola Canada, each of which donated 250,000 soft drinks; McDonald's Canada, which gave hundreds of burgers and $41,000 in cash; Canada Safeway, which gave $200,000 in groceries and provided refrigerated trucks to deliver them; Canadian Tire, which provided 20 semis as warehouse space for donations; and the Royal Bank and Manitoba credit unions, each of which gave a $100,000 cheque. Thomson Corp., proprietors of the *Free Press*, donated $50,000.

Not everything the Salvation Army or Red Cross was offered was easy to use, but there was little they turned down.

Harry Rosen clothing stores donated $65,000 in suit jackets and dress shirts. "Brand-new clothing is a wonderful bonus for people who have been through so much," Bennett said loyally. A livestock farmer in southern Manitoba offered 100 emus for the tables of flood refugees. That was one of the few offers the Sally Ann rejected. It would have cost $50 each to slaughter the big birds. Besides, said

Donations on their way from Windsor, Ont.

Bennett, tongue in cheek, "I didn't want a lot of emu blood on my hands."

The flow of gifts from all over the country was touching.

"It has been incredible the amount of assistance we have received from beyond the borders of Manitoba," Bennett said. "It has been wonderful and inspirational."

The Toronto Blue Jays collected money for flood victims. The Calgary Philharmonic Orchestra put on a benefit concert. George H. Luck elementary school in Edmonton gathered toiletries and shipped them to Winnipeg. In New Glasgow, N.S., residents signed a sandbag as they made donations. The Red Cross sent both bag and cash to Manitoba, realizing the power of the symbolic gesture as well as the practicality of cash.

Among the donations was $1.5 million from the Saguenay region of Quebec, where flash floods caused havoc a year before. Manitoba had given generously then, and now it was harvesting the bread it had cast on those waters.

"I just can't believe people have responded with such kindness," said 32-year-old Ellen Simpson, who lost a barn and the bottom floor of her home just south of Morris.

Gary Filmon said he had always expected Canadians would respond to Manitoba's disaster, but the extent of their generosity amazed him. "This is the essence of Canada," Filmon said. "People saw a need and came to our rescue, our need."

Long after the crisis passed, the help kept pouring in. Warehouse space became the Salvation Army's biggest need. "We've got 40 trailers waiting to be off-loaded in Winnipeg," a Salvation Army officer said in late June. "There's no warehouse space." And there were truckloads of goods all over the country, waiting for word that there was room to unload in Winnipeg, said Luginbuhl.

Some donors were particularly inventive. Two such were Leslie and David Goodwin, of Kelowna, B.C. Using the Internet, they were following the flood drama on the *Free Press* website and were moved to respond. Early in May, David Goodwin posted this on the site's message board:

"Any family with kids who needs to get away from the madness is welcome here at our house in Kelowna, B.C. Don't know how else to help except to send more bedding . . . Remember the goodness of your fellow citizens in this time of crisis."

The next morning, the downloaded message was in the stack of e-mails, press releases and letters on the *Free Press* city desk. The Goodwins' message went to reporter Melanie Verhaeghe. First, she confirmed that the offer was genuine. It was indeed, Leslie Goodwin told her by phone. "We don't have a lot of money, so we can't send money. But we can open our house," said the Kelowna woman.

But how to pick the deserving family? Anyone would want to go, to give up the mud and backache for an idyllic week on the lake in B.C. The town of Rosenort was particularly hard hit that week, so Verhaeghe called the Rosenort fire hall. Did anyone there know of a family who had felt the flood even more keenly than most? And that's how she met Kurt and Tami Siemens.

The Siemenses, farmers at Rosenort, had lost four months of egg production when their barn flooded and they had to ship their chickens for slaughter. Now their house was gone, too. "The inside will have to be gutted and we'll have to start all over again. I'm set back three to four years from this, I figure," Kurt Siemens said.

Kurt was in Rosenort, helping maintain the ring dike, and Tami was in Swan River, where her parents live. With her were daughter Madisson, four, and son Harley, 18 months.

"It's unbelievable. I can't believe someone would do something for me, for someone they don't even know," Kurt said. "It would be nice and maybe we could get our sanity back. That's really nice of them to think of us in the flood area of the world." When he was sure Rosenort was safe, he would be delighted to go.

The Siemens, a farm family who lost their home and livelihood in Rosenort, took up a generous Internet offer to spend a week with a Kelowna family.

Next, Verhaeghe called Greyhound Air. There was this family in Kelowna, the fledgling airline's home, offering a holiday to a flood-stricken Manitoba family of four. Could the airline donate four tickets?

Make it six, said Greyhound, and bring along a reporter and photographer.

By June 4, the water had dropped and Rosenort was safe. What was left of Kurt and Tami's home had emerged from the mud-brown water: a shell of studded walls and the concrete floor of the basement. They flew to Kelowna for their mini-vacation. The city of 90,000 was caught up in the Goodwins' generous offer. The Mediterranean Market delicatessen gave a lunch, the Water Street Grill had the families for dinner. David Goodwin restores toys, especially Barbie dolls, to four-year-old Madisson's delight.

"It's just like we've known each other forever. We just sort of clicked right away," said Leslie Goodwin. "We sat up far too late and talked."

The Siemenses flew back to Manitoba June 9 to begin rebuilding their house and farm. They are expecting guests in the summer of 1998. The Goodwins, who couldn't have found Rosenort on a map six months ago, are coming from Kelowna to visit.

It seemed like everybody wanted to help. Bruce Cockburn, the folk singer, played a concert in early May at Pantages Theatre. The proceeds went to flood relief and 200 seats were set aside, free, for refugees.

The venerable rock band KISS, at the Winnipeg Arena for concerts April 27 and 28, had T-shirts made up that said "KISS Winnipeg We Will Survive." Proceeds from the $32 shirts went to flood relief.

Celtic folk-rockers Leahy, performing at the West End Cultural Centre, gave up their share of the $12 ticket price to flood relief. So did their opening act, Laura Smith. Country singer Michelle Wright had been scheduled to perform at the Walker Theatre on May 5.

"It's unbelievable. I can't believe someone would do something for me, for someone they don't even know."

KURT SIEMENS

Instead, she put off the show to May 26 and set aside the $20 seats in the theatre's upper balcony for flood relief.

Peter Gzowski, in his last season at CBC Radio's Morningside, staged a national benefit concert dubbed the Red River Rally. Performers ranged from Murray McLauchlan, who sang his 1970s ballad called Red River Valley, to Valdy, who was up half the night composing a new song, As the Waters Fall. "I went through 1,500 tune titles last night," Valdy told Gzowski. "I couldn't come up with anything appropriate so I wrote this tune." In it, the veteran of several Winnipeg folk festivals described Canadians as a scattered but caring nation whose sole intention is "to help those in trouble as the rivers rise." Rock superstar Alanis Morissette of Ottawa called CBC Toronto from New Delhi wondering if it was too late for her to get on the show. It was.

The radio concert ended with a group rendition of O Canada. "It was just, oof," said Gloria Bishop, Morningside's executive producer, describing the emotional effect of the patriotic finale. "Even Peter. He promised years ago never to sing on the air."

Within an hour of the concert's end, it had raised $250,000. The pledge lines stayed open for a week and took in $1.5 million.

The May 2 concert was beamed via Radio Canada International to about 2,000 soldiers serving around the world in Bosnia, Haiti, Golan Heights and other areas. It was also aired live on CBC Radio's Internet site to computer users around the world. And on the regular AM band, it beamed into the radio of a car on the Trans-Canada Highway in Alberta.

Singer Tom Jackson got the ball rolling for the Red River Relief concert.

At the wheel was Tom Jackson, the singer, songwriter and actor. Winnipeg is Jackson's home town, but he hadn't been there for much of the flood. He'd been in Calgary, where his CBC-TV drama, North of 60, is shot. He was on his way to Calgary that morning and tuned in Morningside.

"I was listening to Peter's show and I had to pull over to the side of the road because I was so moved I couldn't drive," Jackson said. "I decided this might be another of my moments of calling." In that moment, the Red River Relief concert was born.

Jackson is no stranger to organizing benefits. He is renowned for his annual Christmas-season Huron Carole concerts, which raise money for food banks. And a few days before Gzowski's radio concert, Jackson had produced a fund-raiser at the Calgary Saddledome, raising $600,000. But on the side of the highway in Alberta, he was thinking of something far bigger.

Veteran CBC radio host Peter Gzowski staged a nationwide benefit concert on the airwaves, raising $1.5 million for flood relief.

Jackson had the ball rolling for Red River Relief by the next day, when he called Winnipeg music agent Gilles Paquin. Together, Jackson's Calgary office and Paquin, along with some help from the CBC, assembled a lineup over the following week. The show would be at The Forks in Winnipeg, on Sunday, May 17.

Jackson's past charity work paved the way; he knew who to call and the performers and technicians he called were ready to help.

He got a stage from Regina, a television mobile remote truck from Edmonton and audio equipment from Toronto. About 500 volunteers turned the vacant field north of the Forks Market into a concert venue and broadcasting site.

One of the first performers on board was Burton Cummings, now living in Los Angeles. In the '60s and '70s, the Winnipeg-based Guess Who, with Cummings singing and playing piano, was one of the top rock bands in the world. In April, Cummings had talked of organizing a relief concert. But he cheerfully admitted he didn't have Jackson's

Burton Cummings (below) was one of the first performers on board for the benefit.

The site near the Forks Market was jammed with fans (left and below) on the night of the concert.

Susan Aglukark (left) was among the talent that came from across the country.

149

Randy Bachman and Cummings reunited on stage with a pair of Guess Who classics.

Marc Gallant

organizing skills, and he signed on for Red River Relief.

So did Cummings' old Guess Who bandmate, guitarist Randy Bachman. Bachman and Cummings had reached the pinnacle of rock stardom together, but Bachman was a devout Mormon while Cummings was a devout hedonist. They fell out over Cummings' dissipation and the band split up. Now the two might play together again on Jackson's show.

After the Guess Who, Bachman had scored another success with Bachman-Turner Overdrive, and his partner in that enterprise, Fred Turner, was on the Red River Relief stage. So was Jackson. Celine Dion wasn't there, but contributed a pre-taped segment. Perennial kids' favourite Fred Penner was there, as was newcomer Chantal Kreviazuk. So were the Wyrd Sisters, Susan Aglukark, Amy Sky, John Morgan, George Fox and more.

But the showstoppers were Bachman and Cummings.

They did two songs. First was a stripped-down version of the Guess Who classic Undun. Bachman strummed an electric guitar while Cummings sang and provided a spine-tingling flute solo. Backstage, Bachman said the two had been almost in tears when they'd played it at a soundcheck in the afternoon. "Undun was touching," he said. They closed with American Woman, their 1970 rocker that pushed the Beatles from the top of the charts. Cummings left the stage misty-eyed and the two said they would get together again, soon, probably at Bachman's studio in White Rock, B.C.

"I really do think we'll do something. I really do," Cummings said backstage.

By the end of the night, the six phone lines at CBC had recorded $1.8 million in pledges. The number went over $2 million in the days to come. The unofficial stars of the show were the dozens of Canadian Forces personnel in attendance. They were heartily cheered whenever they were mentioned by onstage performers. "This is the end of a good experience," Pte. Daniel Renaud of the Second Service Transport Battalion in Petawawa, Ont. said while hunched up against a fence with comrades near the stage.

The swarm of armed forces aircraft had now shrunk to just one helicopter, and it circled over the bandstand in the gathering twilight.

There were still sandbags to move, washed-out roads and bridges to replace, flooded houses to be rebuilt. But Bachman's soaring guitar said the worst had been here, and been faced and been beaten.

The sign said it all (above) as did Bachman, Jackson and Cummings (left).

151

Chapter Eleven
GRANDE POINTE

L IKE A rat, the Red River flood got in a dying bite. It took that bite at Grande Pointe, a suburb bordering on Winnipeg's southeast city limits, near where a culvert takes the Seine River through the floodway. In three desperate days in early May, more than 100 Grande Pointe home-owners saw muddy water pour into their houses just when it seemed the end was in sight.

Before the flood, Grande Pointe was home to 150 families. The houses ranged from modest bungalows to spreads that cost more than $200,000. Most of the homes had already survived a major flood – nearly 100 of the houses in Grande Pointe were built before 1979.

Until 1979, there had been no rules about the elevation of homes. After the 1979 flood, the Water Resources Branch recommended that future houses have their foundations between 771 and 772 feet above sea level. The province passed legislation that year requiring that eleva-tion for most homes in the area, but there was nothing the province or the Rural Municipality of Ritchot could do to enforce it. The deci-sion on elevation was ultimately up to the homeowner. Building inspectors would not shut down a construction site because it didn't conform to elevation standards. Still, most people heeded the recom-mendation when they built.

When Elmer Hywarren prepared to build his house on Beauchemin Road, he found his lot was at 763 feet. It cost him $1,000 a foot to haul in enough fill to raise his foundation to 771 feet, but he did it.

When Marian Widla built in Grande Pointe in 1995, he went Hywarren one better, filling his building site to 772 feet.

Arthur Toews built on Carriere Road in 1987. He took note of the building code and ignored it. He felt 769 feet was high enough, based on history. "It was plenty high – much, much higher than 1950," he said.

Of the three neighbours, two would lose their houses in the first week of May.

Looking at the snowdrifts in early April, Bob Stefaniuk and his

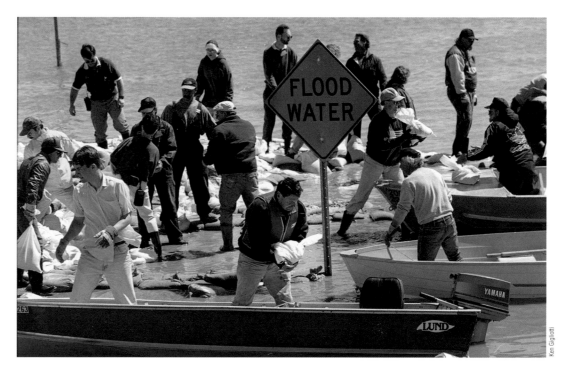

council in Ritchot figured on high water, but not more than they could handle. Some houses would likely need a ring of sandbags for extra protection, maybe six inches or a foot high. The council ordered 100,000 sandbags, an outlay of about $165,000. For a local govern-ment whose entire annual budget is just $2.5 million, it was a signifi-cant bill. If they needed more, their supplier told the councillors, there was an unlimited supply.

That changed on April 19 when Grand Forks was destroyed. There was an instant run on sandbags. Up and down the river, municipalities that had stockpiled bags by the tens of thousands were ordering them a million at a time. By April 20 or 21 there was none to be had.

Volunteers (above) worked at break-neck speed trying to secure area homes. City hydro worker Barry Gembey (opposite) ensures pumps in Grande Pointe are still functioning.

And then came the water. Grande Pointe was dry on Tuesday, April 22. By Thursday, much of the suburb was under a foot of water. It seemed to be coming from every direction.

Some people thought the water was merely runoff from nearby fields and ditches. Others wondered if it came from the Seine River or even the Red River Floodway, just three kilometres to the north.

On Monday, April 21, Hywarren had lined up at the municipal office with about 20 other people. He was there to request 4,000 sandbags and five truckloads of sand – 45 yards of it. The water had already begun to rise at the back of his property and he had emptied his shed. The municipality put his name on a list.

Between Tuesday and Wednesday of that week, the water surged up more than five feet. One tandem of sand arrived. A neighbour brought him two bundles of sandbags. There were supposed to be 1,000 bags in a bundle, but these had only 500. He called the municipal office and asked for more sand.

It was chaos at the office. Debbie Petryk, another Grande Pointe homeowner, phoned in to see if the suburb was going to be evacuated. Call this number, said the man at the other end of the line. "Who should I ask for?" said Petryk. Ask for God, said the man at the municipal office, and hung up.

On Thursday, a Sandbagger machine was at work at the corner of Highway 59 and Provincial Road 300. But it was too late to truck the filled bags into Grande Pointe – the houses, elevated from the surrounding plain, were already islands. The bags had to be taken in by boat, 10 or 15 at a time.

Hywarren set doggedly to work. He put 10,000 sandbags around his house. The first 1,000 were the bags his neighbour brought him. The other 9,000 came in by boat.

On Friday, the RCMP came through Grande Pointe and ordered everybody out. Hywarren complied, but early the next week, he boated back in to his sandbagged house. This time, he vowed he would stay until he could walk out on dry land.

The crisis came to Grande Pointe as suddenly and perplexingly as the overland flooding of April 23. It was the morning of Friday, May 2.

There was more water coming down the Red River than any living person had ever seen. Behind the primary dikes in Winnipeg, the river was at its maximum allowable level – 24.5 feet at the James Avenue pumping station. Any more water and the city's dikes were likely to fail, with incalculable consequences. The floodway was already pushing the limits of its designed capacity, but that couldn't be helped. It would have to take more water.

There was more water coming down the Red River than any living person had ever seen.

Joe Bryksa

Ed Hallama's 100-year-old photographs were among the valuables damaged when the river swept into his Grande Pointe home.

In a scene reminiscent of Dunkirk, a flotilla of boats surrounded Grande Pointe

Doug and Marie-Paule Lemoine at work (above).

A Zodiac brings in yet another load of sandbags.

It was a wet trek finding a way into the community.

Natural Resources raised the floodway gates to push another 7,000 cubic feet per second into Duff's Ditch, raising its flow to 64,000 cfs, the most it had ever carried. It was designed to carry a maximum of 60,000 cfs. The department's calculations said raising the gates would raise the water level in Grande Pointe by six inches. The suburbanites would have to handle it; the alternative was to risk bursting dikes in Winnipeg.

But the water didn't creep up by six inches at Grande Pointe; it came roaring up by several feet. All that afternoon and into the night, boats shuttled back and forth between the Sandbagger and the houses that dotted the great sheet of water covering Grande Pointe. It looked like Dunkirk in 1940.

"I don't think the officials exactly knew what was going on," said Elmer Hywarren. "They've bungled it here as they did in Ste. Agathe. They had their computer models and obviously their computer models were not right. They got caught short in Ste. Agathe and now they've been caught short here."

Said his neighbour, Claude Lemoine: "We're paying the price for protecting the city. They've given up on us. They're using us as their catch basin."

Was that true? Had Grande Pointe been sacrificed to spare the Winnipeg dikes? That was the main question when Larry Whitney had his daily meeting with reporters that Friday afternoon.

Whitney's explanation sounded like the province had made a sort of Sophie's Choice – picking which of two children was to survive. "You're always worried, when you've got two kids, which is being favoured," he told reporters.

But he repeated that the raising of the floodway gates accounted for only six inches of the rise at Grande Pointe. He was at a loss to explain the rest. "Remember how the last few days we talked about how water is going in unpredictable flow patterns?" he asked. He said the losses in Grande Pointe were a defeat for the province's emergency operations. "When you hear what's happened in Grande Pointe, you feel kind of lousy – you feel for those people," he said.

One by one that afternoon, defeated families boated out to Highway 59. The water had come up faster than they could bring in sandbags and pile them up. But the boats kept shuttling back and forth long after dark.

The *Free Press's* lead story the next day was about the flooding at Grande Pointe. The headline, based largely on the provincial press conference, read: Suburb sacrificed to spare Winnipeg.

It was a choice of words that was much debated later, both in and out of the newsroom. It had seemed an accurate reflection of that day's

and night's events, but it may have fanned the mistrust of the government that flared up in Grande Pointe. The editors were satisfied that Winnipeg's safety would be and was given priority over Grande Pointe's, but the suburb had not been deliberately destroyed for the city's sake. For the first time in the flood drama, the *Free Press* felt it had slipped.

Marian Widla's house, built to the government's specifications, flooded. He had a full basement and nearly two feet on the main floor. So did Arthur Toews' place, built two feet lower than spec. But what difference would it have made if he'd built the extra two feet, he angrily demanded later. Your floor is no wetter under three feet of water than it is under one.

The floodway gates were raised again Saturday and Sunday, eventually forcing a record 65,100 cubic feet of water a second into the floodway channel. Elmer Hywarren fought on, and days later, he kept his promise to himself. He walked out of his house. But in a community of 150 homes, his was one of only 25 that escaped the flood.

By Monday, the water had begun to go down, and it did so steadily from then on. For Grande Pointe, the cliche was true: It was all over but the shouting.

That took place at a raucous meeting in Winnipeg's International Inn on Tuesday, May 6. About 500 Ritchot homeowners from Ste. Agathe and Grande Pointe jammed one of the hotel's ballrooms.

Steve Topping, director of the Water Resources Branch, had prepared some slides and tried to use an overhead projector to tell the crowd what had happened.

The sudden rise in Grande Pointe had been unpredictable, he tried to say. The river had risen so high that it ran over a submerged CP Rail track near Niverville that had always held back the water in the past. The water then channelled north along a raised stretch of track

Marc Gallant

Efforts continue (opposite) to thwart the oncoming Red.

One homeowner managed to save his snowmobile atop a car.

Joe Bryksa

Silt marks clearly show how high the water was in Paul Brule's home (above)

Local residents (right) had to use oars when the water became too shallow for the boat's engine.

that runs parallel to Highway 59. The elevation of the track kept floodwater from rejoining the river and instead sent it straight into Grande Pointe, raising the water level there by three feet instead of the six inches that could be attributed to the floodway gates.

The crowd was having none of it. "Before this flood happened, as a resident of RM of Ritchot in 1979, I could have told you that water was going to go over the track. Where were you guys?" a woman screamed at Topping. "Why didn't you know it was going through the six-foot culverts under that track?" "I can't answer that," he replied.

The topic turned to compensation. Would they be fully reimbursed for their losses? Ben Sveinson, the area's member of the legislature, couldn't promise any improvement on the existing flood compensation formula – a $20,000 deductible and a $100,000 maximum. That meant there were people in the ballroom who had total damage to $200,000 houses and would get no more than $80,000. They were angry and they got even angrier later that week, when Gary Filmon said people who choose to build on a flood plain have to be prepared to accept some of the risk involved.

158

Marc Gallant

LOTS FOR SALE

CAMPEAU REAL ESTATE LTD.

From the first stirring of the Red so many weeks ago, people had marvelled at the efficiency of the government and civil servants. They saw people like Alf Warkentin and Larry Whitney working around the clock and they saw the miracle the Highways Department brought forth at the Brunkild dike. But now, for the first time, people were seeing the government as bungling, stingy and cold-hearted.

A barge brings in a huge load of sandbags (above).

Water seeps over an area scrapyard (right).

Cecile Gousseau and Jean-Rene Nicolet (opposite) leave their home on Bartmanovich Road; the dike is still holding.

Chapter Twelve
FREE PRESS COVERAGE

EIGHT MEN sat down for dinner in a north Winnipeg restaurant on the evening of March 25. Nicholas Hirst, who had been appointed editor of the *Free Press* the previous November, had called together some of the newsroom's senior editors. Hirst, 48, wanted to raise three issues and give them a fuller exploration than was possible in the hurly-burly atmosphere that surrounded putting out the daily paper.

There were three stories coming up, he thought, where the *Free Press* could distinguish itself. One was the federal election, which the paper's political reporters expected at the time to be called April 26, as indeed it was. What could the newsroom staff do that would make the paper a must-read for anyone interested in the election? Another story was the inner city, plagued by gangs and street crime but still home to people who were neither criminals nor friends of the gangs. But this world on our doorstep had its doors nearly closed to the news media. How could the *Free Press* be the first to get inside?

And third was the flood that was forecast for the coming spring. How many reporters and photographers would be detailed to cover it? What resources would they need?

Around the table were Hirst; Brian Cole, the editor of the editorial page; Jim Carr, the features editor; John Douglas, the city editor; John Sullivan, the assistant managing editor; Paul Samyn, tagged to move to Ottawa as the *Free Press's* national reporter after covering the federal election; Jon Thordarson, the photo editor; and Buzz Currie, an assistant city editor. Hirst was chairman; Douglas took notes. Three plans emerged:

Currie would head up the election coverage and the *Free Press* would sponsor a series of town hall meetings, at least one in each urban constituency. For the inner city, Carr and Hirst would consider a proposal by freelancers Mike Maunder and Virginia Maracle to write a wide-ranging series of stories that would get beneath the surface of the core area.

Douglas would head up the coverage of the flood story. Manfred Jager, a reporter with a flair for technical subjects, would be assigned to do an explanatory piece on how the Red River Floodway works. Gordon Preece, the art director, would do a detailed graphic to accompany it. Sullivan would arrange the necessary space to run the feature – the two centre pages of a Saturday front section. There would be four-colour process available for Preece's graphics and the centre position meant the piece could be run across the whole two-page spread – what printers call a double truck. Thordarson would get four-wheel-drive trucks, boat trailers, boats and motors and make arrangements to hire the helicopters and airplanes the photographers would need. Sullivan would add to the newsroom's stock of cellular telephones and laptop computers.

The diners adjourned with Douglas undertaking to circulate the minutes back at the office the next morning. Paradoxically, the events of the next two months were vastly different from the way the editors had envisioned them, and yet Douglas's memorandum served as a foundation for what was to come. What lay ahead was, for the people at the table and dozens more back at the *Free Press's* third-floor newsroom on Mountain Avenue, the biggest story of their lives.

That story picked up speed less than two weeks later, when the blizzard struck southern Manitoba and North Dakota. The paper had been producing stories about the co-operative nature of the weather; there was a felicitous stretch of warm weather in Manitoba while the upper reaches of the Red remained frozen. If that continued, Manitoba would be better able to handle the rush of water that would descend when the Red broke up. But the blizzard put an end to that trend.

The forecast before the April 5-6 weekend was for a Colorado low-pressure system to blanket the area with snow and pound it with wind. As well, the U.S. National Weather Service was predicting the cresting of the Red at its source in Breckenridge, Minn. Douglas was

Nicholas Hirst
Editor,
Winnipeg Free Press

The Brunkild Z-dike (opposite) was the focus of much newsroom attention when it was unclear if it could be finished in time to meet the advancing water.

faced with the first of thousands of decisions the flood would entail: Time off would become precious in the weeks to come, so should he start off by assigning an extra reporter to work the weekend? He was reluctant, but Murphy's Law is unbending in a newsroom. If something can go wrong, it will go wrong. Kim Guttormson would go to Breckenridge. She would get her car frozen up to the hubs, she would hitch rides with the National Guard and she would be the first *Free Press* reporter to see the flood of '97 in action. Enough reporters, editors and photographers made it in to the Mountain Avenue offices to produce daily papers during the blizzard. Others, storm-stayed, filed stories by computer modem or by old-fashioned telephone dictation. But for the first time anyone could remember, the *Free Press* was unable to deliver an edition. The papers of Sunday, April 6, and Monday, April 7, were delivered together. For the people who had made it in to the office, Sullivan got coffee mugs made up. Blue print on white china proclaimed: I came into work during the BLIZZARD OF '97 and all I got was this coffee mug.

It took Kim Guttormson two weeks to get home from Breckenridge. She followed the crest as it rolled north, slow but powerful. In Fargo, she wrote about the Salvation Army's introduction to the flood of '97, about the frenzy in Fargo when forecasters said the dikes were too low and about a mother and daughter who died with safety in sight.

And on Friday, April 18, the crest led her to Grand Forks, just in time to witness its destruction.

For the *Free Press* newsroom, as for everyone concerned with the flood, Grand Forks was a galvanizing moment. The flood of '97 had been a big story; now it was virtually the only story. John Douglas, the

The story gained momentum when the blizzard struck on April 6.

One of the first pictures (right) out of Grand Forks shows only a hint of the devastation to come.

164

city editor, had committed the 20 reporters at his disposal. The sports department loaned two more, Dave Supleve and Randy Turner. As the Red spilled over its banks in southern Manitoba, they headed south into the Red Sea. In Altona, Supleve hit it off with Walter Semianiw, the lieutenant-colonel commanding 1PPCLI. Semianiw was always able to find room for a reporter and photographer on one of the 10-tonne trucks that were the best way of getting in to the cut-off towns and farms along the Red. In the island town of St. Jean Baptiste, Turner found a similar ally in Flo Beaudette, the reeve of Montcalm rural municipality. Beaudette took to Turner so warmly that when it appeared there would be an evacuation order for all but essential floodfighters, he proposed enlisting Turner in the Montcalm volunteer fire department. It may have been Turner's sense of priorities that won Beaudette over. When he got to St. Jean Baptiste and watched the rising Red cut off road access into town, Turner's thoughts turned to the well-being of the people, himself included, who were holding out behind the dike. "Is there," he asked Beaudette, "enough beer in the hotel?"

Back in Winnipeg, readers deluged Douglas with demands for information. The flood was the kind of story that there was no need to dramatize; the inherent drama was unavoidable. What the newsroom could do was seek out and print hard information. People wanted to know: Am I safe? What lies ahead? What should I do? How can I help?

Douglas set up a link with Whitney at Water Resources to get daily flood elevations at points along the Red. Throughout the crisis, the last chore in putting together every paper was to update a table of levels that ran inside the first section and to make the necessary changes to a map, which ran every day in the first column of the front page, charting the progress of the crest as it bore down on Winnipeg. Other repeating features were lists of what to do if you got an order to evacuate and what to do if your sewer backed up. And almost every day, there was a list of how readers could help: how to volunteer to build dikes, how to donate to flood relief, which agencies needed people to answer the phones.

It's an everyday challenge in a city newsroom to be accurate while still getting the stories, headlines and pictures to the press on time. But the *Free Press* newsroom, from Hirst down, felt the challenge acutely during the flood. Readers' demands – even needs – for information were palpable, and so was the level of tension. It was no time to spread panic.

So it was that Douglas took with a grain of salt the rumours that began to drift into the newsroom on Monday, April 21 – that there was a way for floodwater to get into the La Salle or even the

Flo Beaudette, reeve of Montcalm rural municipality, proposed enlisting Free Press reporter Randy Turner in the local volunteer fire department.

Assiniboine basin. Then, on Wednesday, April 23, the newsroom had its most frightening day.

It started with the province's press conference – the city and the province were each meeting reporters once a day – that afternoon. Larry Whitney said the floodway was now taking in more water than it was designed to hold. But to the reporter, it sounded like he'd said the floodway could not contain the flow of water that was on the way. Back in the newsroom, the reporter posed the question: What did that mean? Manfred Jager, who had made the operation of the floodway his specialty, was blunt. If the floodway failed, he said, the game was up.

There were grim faces that afternoon around the 20-foot table in the boardroom just off the newsroom. It was 4:30 p.m. and the editors were having the second of the two daily meetings where the next day's paper was planned. When the meeting broke up, Hirst lingered at the table with Patrick Flynn, the assistant managing editor whose job it was to produce the paper. They talked about the paper's responsibility to the readers and what it was that readers would most want to know the next day. They agreed that people would want to know how the province and the city were planning to handle what would surely

'If the floodway failed, the game was up.'

MANFRED JAGER

165

be a mass evacuation in the face of the worst disaster the city had ever seen. It is a common conception that editors lust after bad news, but it is a misconception. There was no joy in the *Free Press* newsroom.

Hirst said he would call Gary Filmon and Susan Thompson and offer them each a space on the front page to detail their plans. First to respond was the premier's office. Bonnie Staples Lyon, the aide who had alerted Filmon to the Grand Forks TV pictures four days earlier, said the province knew of no imminent catastrophe. She set up a phone link between Hirst and Larry Whitney. Thompson called later that evening, responding to a voice-mail message from Hirst. She, too, said she knew of no disaster. But by that time, Hirst had already talked to Whitney.

Larry Whitney of Water Resources was a key source for reporters.

Was the floodway failing? No, said Whitney. It was designed to carry 60,000 cubic feet of water per second and although that limit was going to be exceeded, there was a large safety factor. In fact, the floodway was capable of carrying 100,000 cfs, though that would involve blowing out the highway and rail bridges that cross it, and damming the cuts where they go through the upper floodway bank. There was no perception that the flood would reach that extreme, though, and the floodway flow peaked in early May at 65,100 cfs. Then, said Hirst, what about the stories we were hearing about the dike west of the gates being too low? Yes, Whitney allowed, there was going to be a bit of an extension. A dike three to three-and-a-half feet high would extend west of the existing dike.

And what, asked Hirst, was the bottom line? Would the floodway system work, or was there a danger of mass flooding inside the city limits? That was when Whitney searched for words and came up with his classic:

"There will be no Grand Forks here," he told Hirst.

Or would there? The next morning, in the stack of messages that greeted John Douglas at the beginning of each working day, was an e-mail message that filled a whole 8.5-by-11-inch sheet of paper, with the last line trailing over to a new page. It was unsigned. *My husband is in the military*, it began. *The information he is passing on seems much more serious than what Provincial and even Municipal authorities are saying about the likelihood of Winnipeg being flooded. We live in the heart of St. Vital and my husband is preparing for us to move out*

based on what he knows.

The writer said the province was telling the army, but keeping it from the public, that projections showed the floodway would be out-flanked in the area of Sanford and that the city will be flooded and from a totally new direction that nullifies the protections expected to be obtained from the floodway. She said the military was bringing in resources from as far away as CFB Valcartier in Quebec, that more than 2,000 soldiers were on their way to supplement the number already in Manitoba, that a field medical hospital was on the way because the army expected some city hospitals would be flooded and that mobile water purification units were being brought in because military engineers expected the city's water supply to be contaminated for several weeks.

Some of the claims seemed fantastic – nobody in the newsroom could see how the city's water, piped in from distant Shoal Lake, was in danger of contamination. But the e-mail was rich in detail and it had the ring of truth. And the issues it raised were enormous.

Gordon Sinclair Jr., usually the city columnist but now doing double duty as a reporter, got the job of checking out the claims. What he found out from Bob Meating carried ominous echoes of the news-room's anonymous tipster's message. Yes, a field medical hospital was on the way. Yes, water purification units were coming, though not out of fear for the city. Meating was worried that communities like St. Jean Baptiste and Letellier would have no safe source of drinking water. Yes, there were more soldiers on the way, including the Royal 22nd Regiment from its base in Valcartier.

And topping it all, there was a serious threat in the southwest. That was how the newspaper confirmed on Thursday what Ron Richardson had begun to suspect on Monday – that the flood could find its way over the watershed and into the La Salle basin. The race was on to build the Brunkild dike – not the three-foot mound Whitney had expected on Wednesday, but a mammoth structure that would be Winnipeg's life preserver.

The tipster had put all the right evidence together and come up with the wrong answer. The threat of water running into the La Salle had become the certainty that it would; Meating's concern that the city lacked an evacuation strategy had become the certainty that the city was about to be evacuated. But none of the reporters or editors scorned the anonymous soldier's wife. In the supercharged atmosphere of the oncoming flood, it could happen to anyone.

The flood story had promised from the beginning to be a long one. There was simply no point in dwelling every day on the immensity of the threat and the depth of the water, the angle the national news

Editors thought the public's appreciation for the army was overwhelming.

media took. The *Free Press's* readers already knew they were grappling with a monster. The newsroom's challenge was to deliver facts. People had a need to know what had happened yesterday and what was likely to happen tomorrow. Their greatest and most persistent enemy was fear, and the best antidote for fear was truth. The more correct information the newsroom could supply, the greater would be the trust that residents would put in the assurances that most of them would be safe and there would be no Grand Forks north of the border.

But it was touch and go. For all its news graphics, elevation maps, historical perspectives and details, the newsroom knew there were times that it added to the worry. For 10 days, from April 24 to May 3, Winnipeg was as tense as a bowstring. Like the rest of the city, the *Free Press* newsgatherers felt squeezed in the vise of uncertainty for those 10 days and they shared the euphoria that swept in when the threat was gone.

The editors at the daily 4:30 p.m. meeting, like the one on April 23 where they believed the city was on the brink of a catastrophe, are there to agree on the three or four stories that rate front-page play. It is a rare day that only two stories are played there and rarer still to have a one-story front page. But Wednesday, May 14 was such a paper. The story was the impromptu military parade through town as much of the armed forces contingent, its work finished, boarded trains on Tuesday to return to their home bases. It seemed to the editors that the public's gratitude to the army was overwhelming. The crowd that stood in a cold, misty rain to wave flags and shout thanks bore that out. So the front page carried a big photograph, showing the parade coming down Portage Avenue to Main Street, and a story about the send-off. The headline was simple.

"Thank-you," it said.

Chapter Thirteen
THE AFTERMATH

GARY FILMON felt badgered beyond endurance. A scrum of reporters hemmed him in on every side. The premier was in the hallway outside the Manitoba legislative chamber and it was Friday, June 27. The flood was history, the water gone for more than a month. But it seemed nobody was celebrating survival, or praising the government for its undeniably superb performance during the crisis. Instead, Filmon was enduring his fourth straight day of questions about flood compensation.

The maximum cheque the province was prepared to cut for a homeowner, farmer or business person was $80,000 – the difference between the $100,000 maximum allowable claim and the $20,000 deductible that would be the responsibility of the claimant. That meant a huge loss for the owner of a $250,000 house in Grande Pointe. In the week leading up to Filmon's Friday scrum, there had been rumblings that the province would be more generous with such homeowners. But Filmon was denying it. And he was denying it with a choice of words that seemed designed to alienate every flood victim in the Red River Valley.

"In some cases, people chose to live outside the city for lifestyle to avoid higher taxes and they pay no premiums and now they are having a lot of money paid to them by the taxpayer at large," Filmon said.

The reporters were confused. Why, they wondered, would Filmon condemn a sizable block of voters as whining tax-dodgers when accommodating them would cost him virtually nothing? Above a $5-million threshold, the federal government would pay 90 per cent of the flood-relief bill. So Filmon was, in effect, bad-mouthing his constituents to guard Ottawa's budget.

The reporters were also pressing Filmon about the confusing stories that had come out of the cabinet room through the week. And for these, Filmon had nobody to blame but himself. On the Tuesday, Government Services Minister Frank Pitura said the province was

going to ease the burden on people who'd had major losses – either raising the $100,000 ceiling or raising the deductible. The next day, Filmon contradicted his minister.

It went on. On Thursday, Pitura reluctantly revealed the province was planning to waive the deductible for people whose homes were total writeoffs. There were about 40 such homeowners. And on Friday, Pitura said that decision had in fact been made at Wednesday's cabinet meeting.

So why had it been kept secret? Filmon's answer was lame: "I know myself, I assumed that was a decision we had already communicated because I talked about that numerous times out here in scrums in the hall."

Grande Pointe residents (above) took their compensation demands to the provincial legislature in June.

Stretches of Hwy. 75, (opposite) the province's main route south from Winnipeg, were completely washed out.

169

Grande Pointe resident Garry Petryk lost about 80 per cent of his home and most of his business.

Joe Bryksa

170

It was particularly puzzling because the news would have been at least some relief for the beleaguered Pitura, who'd had to face 400 angry valley residents outside the Legislative Building on Thursday night. Shouting, "Show us the money" – playing on the trademark phrase from Jerry McGuire, a popular movie that had just been released – the homeowners hooted as Pitura spoke. "Nice speech," they jeered, and "Where's Filmon?"

Where indeed? He could have spared his colleague Pitura at least some of the crowd's ire by advising him to tell the residents what had already been decided – that there would be some improvement in circumstances for the worst-hit among them.

But that's the way it went in June. The province and the Red Cross had been superb during the crisis. But when the bills came in, the world turned upside down.

Even in Grande Pointe, there was disagreement about where the province's responsibility ended.

While the water was still going down, Grande Pointe resident Bob Wosner took his huge loss philosophically. His custom metal-working shop was destroyed in the surge of water that struck the community May 2. But, "Nobody owes us anything," he said two weeks later. "People need to start taking some responsibility of their own."

But a block away, his neighbour Garry Petryk viewed a similar loss from the opposite point of view. Petryk, like Wosner, had severe house damage and the loss of the building from which he ran a home-based business – a hauling service in his case. "I want 100 per cent compensation, landscaping, no deductible. Everything," Petryk said. "Natural Resources screwed up and now it's time for them to pay."

It wasn't just that the province was dodgy about how much money people would get; it was slow to get the costs counted. It started the process in May with just 31 assessors and it wasn't until July that it brought in more than 100 more assessors from across the country to speed up the job. Harold Clayton, the EMO director, was defensive. "Anger is a dynamic of an event like this," he said in July. "We knew we were facing that, one way or the other. People, as part of the grieving process, seek a target. If we were there the day after with a construction crew, people still would be angry."

Clayton's frustration may have been heightened by a case of writer's cramp – he had just spent 36 hours signing 3,580 award letters, which flood victims would be able to use as bank collateral as they repaired their stricken homes, farms and businesses. But it had taken six weeks to get the letters ready for Clayton's signature – a long time for someone living in a camper trailer.

The letters, too, sowed confusion. Many of the recipients thought

"Never in a million years would I have expected to have to turn to them for help."

KURT SIEMENS

Father Gerrard Levesque wades into the mess in the basement of his Ste. Agathe church.

171

Marg Waddel surveys the damage to her St. Mary's Road home.

Ken Gigliotti

Angry residents from the R.M. of Ritchot gathered in Winnipeg.

Phil Hossack

Art and Irene Decruyenaere sit among the ruins of their home on St. Mary's Road.

Ken Gigliotti

the amount stipulated in the letter was far less than the real damages. Was it a final offer? Would taking the letter to the bank mean giving up future claims?

Clayton's office, the same agency that had masterminded the battle against the flood of the century, was now bureaucracy at its worst – slow, muddled and afflicted with tunnel vision. The award letters said the amount was a maximum payment, but not what the amount was meant to cover or when the cheque could be expected. The first callers after the letters went out were told that the amount was indeed a final settlement. Later callers were told it was an initial payment, that they would get the balance when they sent in the receipts. But how, homeowners asked, could they be sure the government would approve the money spent on repairs? The EMO hadn't considered that problem. Clayton retreated behind a shield of wounded pride: "I hear people saying, 'I don't trust you,' " he said, "but I've never been dishonest with somebody."

The Red Cross, too, was feeling the heat. Like EMO, its performance during the flood had been top-notch. The Red Cross role had been fund-raising, and by July it was sitting on donations of about $16 million.

So the Red Cross was embarrassed, as well it might be, when it emerged in mid-July that 600 flooded-out families from south of Winnipeg were dependent on the Winnipeg Harvest food bank to feed themselves. One of the recipient families were market gardeners from St. Adolphe who had given produce to Winnipeg Harvest a few years before. "It rips another part of your heart out," said one of the farmers. "Never in a million years would I have expected to have to turn to them for help."

The problem, said Harvest director David Northcott, was that people had used up all their savings and credit to get themselves housed again. They were afraid that winter would be upon them before the province and the Red Cross got the relief cheques out. Now that so much money had been spent on shelter, there was little left for groceries.

"What a mess it is out there," Northcott said. "We've got millions in flood assistance sitting in banks and hundreds of millions promised (from governments) and these people are being told the cheque is in the mail. There is no need for this to have gone this far."

Stung, the Red Cross vowed to do better. It pleaded that it had been overwhelmed by the immensity of the damage. It also pointed out that much of its role was to supplement the aid the province would disburse. It was as frustrated as everyone else with the province's pace, the Red Cross said.

Jake Courcelles examines the wreckage of his father's house in Ste. Agathe.

The flood exposed some surprising gaps in Manitoba's armour.

173

Al Wallice (above) salvages what he can from his flood-damaged house on Red River Drive. Wallice is giving up his home on the Red and selling the property.

The crumbled remains of Hwy. 75 (right).

The province could point an accusing finger, though not as convincingly, toward Ottawa. The federal and provincial governments had signed a memorandum of understanding on May 1, committing themselves to flood prevention measures in Manitoba. Manitobans had begun to despair about that promise, too, when an announcement came in mid-July that Ottawa had contributed $12 million towards the diking and home removal that would have to be done.

The province matched it, setting up a $24-million fund for flood protection. Axworthy said it had taken time to negotiate the aid because it was precedent-setting and the same kind of help would have to go to other provinces if they needed it. The province said flood-proofing the valley to 1997 levels would cost about $44 million, but the $24-million fund was enough to go with because the work could not all be done in a year.

Though his bulldog approach had strained relations with Ottawa, it appeared Filmon had carried the day on flood prevention measures. The federal formula, which Filmon had attacked early during the election campaign as stingy and short-sighted, was now altered in Manitoba's favour. The works would take time – it had taken until 1982 to bring the dikes up to the 1979 level. But Manitoba would enter the 21st century with a system of dikes and ditches that should be proof against whatever the Red can bring in the century to come.

The flood exposed some surprising gaps in Manitoba's armour, and some of those will have to be addressed at the same time as the ring dikes are heightened and houses are raised on extra landfill. For example, Alf Warkentin will have to start training a backup or two in his arcane, but stunningly accurate, science of flood forecasting. As well, it emerged that neither the city nor the province had a topographical map. Such a map would have told the province much earlier that there was a low point near Brunkild, and the wild – and expensive – scramble to build the Z-dike would have been eased.

And it became clear after the flood that nobody had given much thought to how its victims were to be aided.

But those faults should not diminish what was accomplished. There was, as Larry Whitney predicted, "no Grand Forks here." There were, regrettably, three lives lost to the flood in Manitoba. But none were because of failed dikes or bungled evacuations. For a month, the Canadian military turned the valley into a battle zone, with land, marine and air missions night and day. Yet, in all that risky business, none of the 8,500 combatants died. Ste. Agathe and Grande Pointe flooded, but those communities and the farms that were flooded up the valley don't come close to matching the destruction in Grand Forks.

Evelyn Vien stands amid the ruins of her Grande Pointe home.

175

Best of all was what Manitoba learned about itself. It is a province of rugged fighters. It and its capital city have civil services that can work miracles when the chips are down. It is a part of a generous country, one that puts aside its squabbles in a time of need. It is the province where the Canadian military will long remember the rebirth of its proud reputation.

And Manitoba is a survivor. The Red River is a fact of life in the province. It led to Manitoba's early settlement and provincehood, and it is the giver of the fertile soil that makes the valley prosper. It is the mother of Manitoba. Sometimes, as in the spring of 1997, Manitoba's mother will be an angry old sow, driven so mad by blizzards and rains that she tries to devour her children.

She has tried before and will try again. The greatest legacy of the flood of 1997 is the certainty that she will never succeed.

In the pale light of dawn – months after the mighty Red roared – the river remains a reminder of nature's uncompromising power.

Wayne Glowacki

Statistics

Ken Gigliotti

WATER LEVELS

Various authorities have preferences for recording river water levels differently.

For instance, in the United States, the Red River levels are listed in feet above river bottom. That is, the Red at Grand Forks crested at 54 feet above river bottom.

The Manitoba Government prefers to record river levels in feet above sea level. For example, the Red River crested at Emerson at 792.5 feet above sea level. That allows homeowners to check provincial files for their property elevation to determine how high they must build their dikes.

Within Winnipeg, the river level is recorded according to its height at the James Avenue pumping station above the normal winter ice level. That is, the Red crested at 24.5 feet above winter ice levels.

Imperial measurement is the choice of hydrologists, who claim it is easier to work with.

River measurements in centimetres are too small, and metres are too big. If river levls are projected to be two to four feet above year-ago levels, in metric it becomes 0.66 metres to 1.33 metres.

Index